BITCOIN

& THE FUTURE OF FUNDRAISING

A Beginner's Guide to Cryptocurrency Donations

ANNE CONNELLY
& JASON SHIM

Bitcoin and the Future of Fundraising: A Beginner's Guide to Cryptocurrency Donations by Anne Connelly and Jason Shim

ISBN-13: 978-1-7774703-0-2

For information on distribution, translations, bulk sales, or permission requests, please contact Innoraise Imprints directly:

Innoraise Imprints
PO Box 98133 Carlaw
Toronto, Ontario M4M 1J0
Canada

www.innoraiseimprints.com
info@innoraiseimprints.com

TABLE OF CONTENTS

About the Authors

Anne Connelly is passionate about harnessing blockchain and cryptocurrencies to transform the lives of people around the world. Anne is Faculty at Singularity University, teaching global leaders how exponential technologies can solve problems that impact over a billion people. Anne previously worked with Doctors Without Borders as a field worker in Central Africa, as a fundraiser in their Canadian and Irish offices, and as a member of the board of directors. As the Director of Fundraising at Dignitas International, Anne set up one of the world's first Bitcoin donation programs. In 2015, she was given the AFP New Fundraising Professional Award. Anne has a Bachelor of Life Sciences from Queen's University, an MBA from McMaster University, and is certified in Strategic Disruption from Harvard Business School. She was honoured as one of CBC's 12 Young Leaders Changing Canada and one of the Fifty Most Inspirational Women in Technology in Canada.

Jason Shim loves to explore the question, "How can we harness technology to make a difference in the world?" As Director of Digital Strategy and Transformation, Jason has led technology and innovation at Pathways to Education Canada, an organization dedicated to helping youth in low-income communities to graduate from high school and reach their full potential.

With experience spanning the nonprofit and academic sectors both as an employee and a consultant, Jason has consistently helped organizations stay ahead of the technology curve. In 2013, he led Pathways to Education Canada to become one of the first charities to issue tax receipts for Bitcoin donations.

Jason serves as an editor at *Ledger*, a peer-reviewed scholarly journal at the University of Pittsburgh that publishes full-length original research articles on the subjects of cryptocurrency and blockchain technology. In addition, Jason serves on the board of NTEN, an organization dedicated to helping nonprofits fulfill their missions through the skillful and racially-equitable use of technology.

ACKNOWLEDGEMENTS

Anne Connelly

I would like to thank my co-author Jason, my family for supporting my pursuit of cryptocurrencies, and the global blockchain community for their work in developing and sharing this world-changing technology.

Jason Shim

Thank you to my co-author Anne, for the idea around collaborating on a book to support nonprofits who are interested in cryptocurrency. Thanks are also due to: Shub, for introducing me to cryptocurrency; to my colleagues at Pathways to Education for being open to launching a Bitcoin donation program in the early days; to my colleagues at the cryptocurrency journal *Ledger* for the inspiration; and to Elysia, for your endless encouragement, support, and love.

Anne and Jason

We are grateful to our editor, Richard Ford Burley, for his thoughtful and thorough editing of our manuscript. We are also deeply appreciative of the careful review by countless individuals, including Rebecca Davies, Paul Nazareth, Ken Wyman, Jane Cronin, Elysia Guzik, and Nicole Ford Burley. Thanks to Cliff Seto for his design support. Thank you to the fundraisers and philanthropists who interviewed for us, including Alejandro, Andrew, Henah Parikh, Tony Stewart, Connie Gallippi, Jim Carter III, Michael Tozoni, and Ken Wyman. Also, thank you to Beth Kanter, Amy Sample Ward, Brock Warner, Liz Rejman, Konstantinos Stylianou, and Mark Blumberg for generously sharing their wisdom, knowledge, and advice along the way.

Finally, a thank you to *you*, the reader, for taking the time to learn more about cryptocurrency.

If you would like to stay in touch, please visit our website at www.bitcoinfundraising.com to learn more about speaking engagements, webinars, consulting, and updates.

Take a moment to send us a note to say hello—
anne@bitcoinfundraising.com or jason@bitcoinfundraising.com, or take a selfie with the book and tag us on Twitter @Anne_Connelly and @jasonshim.

FOREWORD

BY BETH KANTER

Cryptocurrencies first caught my attention a number of years ago when I was exploring the question, "What's next?" Throughout my career, I have had a keen interest in observing technologies that are on the horizon and considering the implications for the nonprofit sector. In recent years, an emerging, recurring, and important theme has been the potential of blockchains and cryptocurrencies, alongside other technologies such as artificial intelligence and virtual reality.

When considering disruptive technologies, leaders in the nonprofit sector cannot stick their heads in the sand and ignore something as powerful as cryptocurrencies—this is something that will have an impact on fundraising and donations, and on the world at large. The opportunity that cryptocurrencies present, as with any emerging technology, is that folks can get in early and understand it before it becomes more mainstream.

There are often many questions that accompany new technologies. Before social media and crowdfunding were widely adopted, I often heard from organizational leaders in the nonprofit sector who expressed fear and skepticism around these technologies: would there be a return on investment? Was it worth the time and resources? Today, however, the question has moved beyond *if* these technologies should be used to *how* they should be used, and more nonprofits are now confidently using social media and crowdfunding channels to further their missions. There has always been a return on learning over the long term, and organizations composed of people who are consistently improving are well-suited for adapting to the future.

Looking ahead, my hope is that organizational leaders do not opt out of the opportunities that emerging technologies present. There is an inherent risk in learning about and applying new technologies, but it can pay off over the long term. The future is rarely perfect and things may not always work 100%, but when combined with an openness to learning and continuous improvement, as Anne and Jason put it, organizations can "future-proof against uncertainty and lost opportunity."

Nonprofits are still in the early adopter stage when it comes to cryptocurrencies. The value in learning more is that it can help you identify your next steps in determining how the technology can be used to serve stakeholders. Executive education can help lift barriers to adoption and guide understanding. Paying attention to future tech trends and how they may influence your nonprofit is an important strategic consideration. While it doesn't mean you have to immediately hire a director of cryptocurrency fundraising, being educated and informed is important.

Clay Shirky observed that, "Communications tools don't get socially interesting until they get technologically boring." Similarly, as cryptocurrencies eventually become more mainstream, more socially interesting applications will emerge. However, as we move ahead, issues of bias and inequity do not disappear with technology. Just as considerations of algorithmic discrimination need to be considered with AI, nonprofits also need to consider the role that inclusion may play in shaping how cryptocurrencies may be used to meet their missions more effectively. Nonprofits have a role to play in ensuring that technology is used in equitable ways; in order for that to happen, organizational leaders need to ensure they are knowledgeable and seek out executive education and professional development in these areas.

When learning about new technologies, it is always helpful to have a cogent and well-researched resource that can get you up to speed on a complex topic.

For many years, Anne and Jason have worked in nonprofit organizations and have been speaking and writing about cryptocurrencies and the future. Their passion for the topic has been evident in their efforts to share their expertise, experience, and knowledge with others in the nonprofit sector. *Bitcoin and the Future of Fundraising* is a useful guide to learn about cryptocurrency fundraising and provides great value to nonprofit leaders who are looking to future-proof themselves and their organizations.

As we continue to explore the question of "What's next?" for nonprofits, don't opt out of the future, jump in and create it.

Beth Kanter
Trainer, Virtual Facilitator and Author
Co-author, *Measuring the Networked Nonprofit*
Co-author, *The Happy, Healthy Nonprofit*
www.bethkanter.org
Twitter: @kanter

Preface

This book started as a conversation about possibilities, centered around the question, "What is stopping fundraisers from getting involved in Bitcoin?"

Nonprofits are a powerful force for good and play a critical role in serving the public interest; however, in order for organizations to fully realize their missions, it's critical that technology is also recognized and used as an impact multiplier. As a technology, cryptocurrency has transformed from an idea to a global phenomenon in just a short time and nonprofits have an opportunity to be a part of this.

We began writing this book at the beginning of 2020 and as the year unfolded, so did a global pandemic, which upended many underlying assumptions about the world. This has had an impact on how we work, how we learn, and how we fundamentally interact with others. The world experienced a rapid and unprecedented shift in technology use and, in some ways, the future arrived ahead of schedule.

Regardless of COVID-19, we are living in a reality of constant change. While we remain hopeful about the future, we also recognize that we, as leaders and fundraisers, need to play an active role in shaping this new reality by expanding opportunities for nonprofits.

We've both shared our knowledge of cryptocurrencies over the years in efforts to help organizations grow, adapt, and future-proof against uncertainty and lost opportunity. Our intention in writing this guide is not to predict the future, but to create it with you—and this book serves as an invitation.

We invite you to join us and to get excited about the possibilities presented by cryptocurrency fundraising and by the community of donors who want to change the world with you, and are just waiting to be engaged with the right opportunity.

In reading this book, we hope that you will accept our invitation to create the future together.

We Are Not Investment Advisors

You're already doing your own research by reading this book. What we share is based on our own personal and professional experiences; however, we also approach this topic with humility, acknowledging that we are writing about a rapidly-changing environment and what we share is a snapshot. We encourage you to independently research and verify all information you read about crypto, including what you find in this book.

A Lawyer Provided Us With This Paragraph

The content in this publication is offered for informational and educational purposes only. It is not and should not be construed as investment, financial, legal, tax, or other professional advice, and it is not an offer, solicitation, recommendation, or endorsement of any financial products or services. It is also general in nature, and does not consider individual circumstances of any third party. The authors are not licensed investment advisors, make no representations or warranties otherwise, do not accept any responsibility for third-party actions or damages on the basis of the content of this publication, and explicitly encourage readers and third parties to seek professional advice and to evaluate on their own the contents of this publication and the merits and risks of their investment and financial decisions and actions.

INTRODUCTION

"I want to be able to educate and help people— help them prosper. Crypto is helping us do that."

- Tony Stewart, CEO and Co-Founder of Us4Warriors

About a decade ago, charities started receiving requests to take donations of something they had never seen or heard of before—Bitcoin. Early Bitcoin donors tell stories about how, in order to donate, they googled "charities that accept Bitcoin" and chose one from the small handful of organizations that could actually take their donation.

Cryptocurrencies have been all over the news since the invention of Bitcoin in 2008, and their growth shows no signs of stopping. Today, awareness and adoption of Bitcoin and other cryptocurrencies has grown exponentially, and yet the number of charities accepting cryptocurrency donations hasn't. Millions of people worldwide use Bitcoin to send money, spend money, and invest, but when they want to donate, they are presented with few options.

For many people, logging onto the internet for the first time and accessing all of the world's knowledge was a moment of technological magic. In moments like these, there was not only a sense of amazement and wonder, but also one of mysterious awe and anticipation in knowing that there was so much possibility, but not knowing exactly what it would look like.

When it comes to cryptocurrencies, what lies ahead for nonprofits will be a theme of change and adoption. "In the early days of monthly contributions, it meant asking donors for post-dated cheques and setting up physical filing systems each month," shares Ken Wyman, an active fundraiser for over 40 years. "For many years, charities were very reluctant to accept credit cards."

It's hard to imagine a modern donor searching online for "charities that accept credit cards" because usage is so pervasive, but many of the things that are now obvious to us have often been met with skepticism at some point; however, skepticism can evolve into enthusiasm when there is a better understanding of the long-term potential for something new.

Cryptocurrencies are still in their infancy, but their usage is growing. Just as websites and credit card payments have become commonplace among nonprofits, cryptocurrencies will continue to evolve, providing new opportunities to those who are ready to adapt. While fundraisers are generally familiar with the phrase, "You don't get what you don't ask for," when it comes to cryptocurrencies, *you also don't get what you can't accept.*

This book is set up in three sections: *Learn the Basics*, where you will understand what cryptocurrencies are and how to buy and send them; *Setting up your Program*, where you learn how to establish the infrastructure for a successful crypto donation program; and *Getting the Gift*, where you learn about the unique nature of crypto donors and how to secure their gift. Finally, you can read interviews with early crypto pioneers, fundraisers who have crypto donation programs, and crypto donors, to hear their views on the landscape of crypto giving.

By the end of this book, you will have everything you need to set up your own Bitcoin donation program, so that you can capture the opportunity to connect with cryptocurrency donors who are passionate about your cause.

Thank you for joining us on this journey in being an early adopter in the fundraising world.

The Opportunity for Fundraisers

> *"Organizations that are willing to experiment and try, even if they don't realize it yet, have the opportunities."*
>
> - Jim Carter III, Founder of Cause Hack

With new technological advancements, new opportunities for philanthropy emerge. Television broadcasting made it possible to run telethons. Credit card systems and the internet led to crowdfunding. And today, blockchain technology is allowing fundraisers to accept cryptocurrency donations and explore new ways to engage donors.

The success of cryptocurrencies has created a brand new generation of wealthy donors. For some, it began as an exploration of a technological curiosity; for others, it was an investment in a high-risk opportunity. Whatever their individual circumstances, the one thing many early cryptocurrency adopters have in common is that many of them suddenly found themselves with newfound wealth.

To understand the opportunity this has created for fundraisers, take a look at the second-largest cryptocurrency platform today, Ethereum. When Ethereum launched in 2014, a single unit of its cryptocurrency, Ether, was valued at $0.30.[1] At its height in January 2018, Ether traded at just over $1,400, which represented a return of over 4,500 times. To put it simply, someone who invested $215 in Ether during the launch would have seen their portfolio grow to $1 million in just four years.

These portfolio gains happened quietly in the background, with many cryptocurrency holders fiercely protecting their privacy. Statistics, however, tell a different story of wider adoption: a 2018 survey on cryptocurrencies found that 89% of Canadians were aware of Bitcoin and 5% owned

[1] All dollar values are in United States Dollars unless otherwise specified.

Bitcoin, which was an increase from 2017.[2] In 2020, the University of Cambridge estimated a total of up to 101 million unique users of cryptocurrency.[3] And this is just the beginning. Recently, PayPal announced that it plans to allow cryptocurrencies as a funding source for purchases at 26 million merchants worldwide.[4] As we write this, the total value of all cryptocurrencies is over $1 trillion and growing.[5]

So why should charities pay attention? Because when polled, less than 4% of charities accept cryptocurrency donations.[6, 7] The wealth is there, but is your nonprofit ready to receive it?

The wealth is there, but is your nonprofit ready to receive it?

It has already been over a decade since the first nonprofit organization began accepting cryptocurrency donations. In January 2011, the Electronic Frontier Foundation announced that it would accept donations in Bitcoin;[8] this prompted the crypto community to get behind the idea of donating. Charities that have been early adopters of cryptocurrency—the ones that appeared in those early search engine results for "charities that accept Bitcoin"—have been afforded a head start on engaging with new crypto-savvy donors. In most cases, their innovation has been met with large donations and deep connections with donors whose engagement continues to grow.

---

[2] Huynh et al., "Benchmarking Bitcoin Adoption in Canada."
[3] Blandin et al., "3rd Global Cryptoasset Benchmarking Study."
[4] PayPal, "PayPal Launches New Service Enabling Users to Buy, Hold and Sell Cryptocurrency."
[5] CoinMarketCap, "Total market capitalization."
[6] Connelly, "The Landscape of Cryptocurrency Donation Programs."
[7] Nonprofit Tech for Good, "Global NGO Technology Report 2019"
[8] Reitman, "Bitcoin - a Step Toward Censorship-Resistant Digital Currency."

One of the first crypto donor initiatives was the Bitcoin100, offering donations of 100 bitcoin to charities that would accept them. During the course of its existence, Bitcoin100 funded over 90 charities. You can read more about Bitcoin100 in the interview with Michael Tozoni.

As the crypto industry and its community started to grow, so did adoption by charities. Pathways to Education Canada became the first Canadian organization to issue a tax receipt for Bitcoin donations in November 2013 and Dignitas International launched a program shortly after, in May 2014. Notable organizations such as United Way, Red Cross, and Save the Children have also announced Bitcoin donation programs; however, the overall number of charities set up with the capacity to accept Bitcoin remains relatively low.

But those who do set up programs are generally successful. Khan Academy, The Water Project, and the Last Door Recovery Centre were among the 80 charities that received a total of 228 bitcoins from the Bitcoin100 donation initiative from 2012-2015. The Internet Archive, ACLU, and Watsi were among the 60 charities that received over $55 million in Bitcoin donations from the Pineapple Fund. Covenant House was the recipient of proceeds from cryptocurrency events like Toronto's Merry Merkle holiday fundraiser, which raised over $200,000 (Canadian), and continued to drive the culture of donating within the crypto community. Future forward organizations are using crypto as an effective way to grow their investment funds. The Silicon Valley Foundation at one point held over $4.5 billion in cryptocurrency assets.

In addition to providing a diversified revenue stream, organizations who adopt Bitcoin are also building organizational capacity around innovation, and have the opportunity to prepare themselves for a future that includes digital currency. For fundraisers, it's an opportunity to anticipate and create the future.

Crypto Philanthropists

Crypto exchange Binance donated $1 million in their BNB token to the Australian Bushfires Donation Project to help fight the forest fires in Australia in 2020.[9]

[9] Mizrahi, "Binance Donates $1 Million in Crypto for Australian Bushfire Relief."

I: Learn the Basics

What Is a Cryptocurrency?

> *"I realized that if we could capture just a small fraction of the value created by this industry to do good, it would have an incredible impact."*
>
> - Connie Gallippi, Founder and Executive Director of BitGive

In the 13 years from 2008 to 2021, cryptocurrency has gone from an idea to a global phenomenon. To begin to understand cryptocurrencies, it's important to start not with how they work, but with why they matter. To do that, we need to look back in history.

When you think back to a time long ago when everyone lived in tiny villages, every transaction a person made was with someone they knew. This familiarity meant that every transaction used something special to make it work: trust. The social consequences of failing to follow through on a payment or repay a loan ensured that others were highly incentivized to honour a deal. This trust among small groups of people made these direct, peer-to-peer transactions possible.

However, as villages grew into cities and global commerce expanded, these transactions built on trust between neighbours just weren't possible anymore. At some point, as numbers grew, people would have to transact with someone they didn't know if they could trust.

This was the beginning of centralized trust providers—groups like governments, banks, and corporations that would sit in the centre of a transaction to provide trust between unknown parties. In many cases, charities and nonprofits fulfill that same role, providing assurance to the donor that their money is being used for its intended purpose to help beneficiaries.

When you think about the financial transactions you make on a daily basis, almost all of them flow through an intermediary. When sending money to friends and family, you use a bank or a payment app instead of directly mailing them cash. When getting a ride to a party, you use Uber or Lyft instead of connecting with the driver directly. When you rent your place out while you're away, you host with Airbnb and receive payment through the platform. These centralized intermediaries ensure that your money gets to its recipient, you don't get into an unsafe vehicle, and your Airbnb guests can't leave without paying. These intermediaries provide trust.

We've built our entire society using these centralized intermediaries. They've enabled us to scale transactions and interactions in a way that previously wasn't possible—but it comes at a cost. Most trust providers take a cut of the transaction or charge a subscription fee, and in the cases where we aren't paying with money, we are paying in other ways. For example, through taxation in the case of land title registries, or in the case of services like Facebook or Google, with access to our data. But the downsides of centralized models aren't all about cost. Centralized trust providers are susceptible to human fallibility. Records can be falsified, corporations can steal and abuse user data,[10] and banks can launder money for cartels.[11] But how can we transact globally, as we need to, without relying on these intermediaries?

To get an idea of how we might disrupt centralization within our society, let's take a look at the computer industry.

In the early days of computer sales, people bought their systems through retail stores. Every sale involved sending the computer from the manufacturer to the retailer who would then sell it to the customer. Then along came Dell, a company whose innovation was allowing people to customize and purchase computers online, removing the need for retailers.

---

[10] Banjo et al., "TikTok's Huge Data Harvesting Prompts U.S. Security Concerns."
[11] Vulliamy, "How a big US bank laundered billions from Mexico's murderous drug gangs."

They were able to do this because the internet allowed them to connect directly with customers in a way that wasn't previously possible. "Disintermediation," as this is called, is exactly what it sounds like: the removal of intermediaries in transactions, in this case, the retail store. This strategy can be very effective at cutting costs. For every intermediary you remove, you remove their markup as well as the complexity of managing another step in the process. You also remove levels of opacity in the transaction and potential risks like fraud.

The key to cryptocurrencies is disintermediation, but on a much greater scale—through the concept of decentralization.

Decentralization is the transfer of power and authority from centralized parties, like a government or a corporation, to individuals. A government that is fully centralized would be a dictatorship, where one single individual would hold absolute power in decision making. By contrast, a fully decentralized government structure would be an inefficient direct democracy, in which each citizen would vote on every single issue. Most countries fall somewhere in the middle, a mixture of centralized and decentralized elements, creating a balance of power between federal, state/provincial, and municipal levels.

Cryptocurrency is the separation of money and state

One major area where governments hold complete centralized control is money. The value of a country's money is managed by, and can be manipulated by, the government—for better or for worse. Money only exists because: (a) the government says it does, and (b) we all agree. This only works when citizens fully trust their governments to manage national financial systems and monetary policy. In some countries, the government is trustworthy and does a good job. In others, the government is neither trustworthy nor competent and the citizens may suffer from extreme inflation, making their salaries and life savings worthless.

This brings us back to our original question, why do cryptocurrencies matter? Cryptocurrency is the separation of money and state.

Crypto Philanthropists

In 2020, BitMEX exchange donated $2.5 million to four organizations fighting COVID-19: a biosecurity program called the Nuclear Threat Initiative, Gates Philanthropy Partners, Our World in Data, and OpenMinded.[12]

[12] Khatri, "BitMEX operator is donating $2.5M to coronavirus relief efforts."

All About Money

> *"I grew up in Greece where they had issues with high inflation. We had to stock our refrigerator with food because at the end of the month your salary wasn't worth very much."*
>
> - Alejandro, Crypto Donor

Imagine, for a moment, your dream vacation destination. Now imagine that you spent ten years collecting airline points, saving them up to turn your dream into a reality. Shopping at inconvenient grocery stores, buying particular brands you might not have otherwise bought, and giving up your data, all to achieve your goal of lying on the beach or hiking up a mountain.

The points program is owned and managed by the local airline in your country and they have control over the whole system. Just as you've reached your goal of getting the 1 million points you need to take your trip, the airline states that now you need 2 million points. In essence, the value of your points dropped by half overnight. You are horrified, realizing that you will need another decade to accumulate the points you need, when you already felt like you'd met the airline's requirements for your trip. You complain to the airline, but because they are in complete control of the points system, they can really do whatever they want. You lose faith in the airline and stop collecting points, as do many other people across the country. You stop shopping for brands that would get you points, and the airline's brand partnerships decline. People can no longer trust the centralized organization that controls the points and the whole system starts to fall apart. Monetary systems work a lot like this. For some, what is described above doesn't require imagination, as it has been a lived reality.

Crypto Lingo

"Fiat" ⟶ Historically, national currencies were backed by assets like gold. A fiat currency is a government-issued currency that isn't backed by anything other than the government's word that its money has value and the trust citizens place in the government's ability to maintain that value. In the crypto community, the term 'fiat' describes what society knows simply as "money." The US Dollar, the Euro, and the Japanese Yen are all examples of fiat currencies.

When you think about money in today's world, it's always connected to one national government or another. In many countries, this gives citizens trust in their financial system. It makes them more likely to use their national currency and believe in its stability as a store of value. In some countries, however, governments that are poor custodians of their own financial systems, through mismanagement or other issues such as conflicts or corruption, cause instability and inflation. If a government can't manage the financial system well, citizens, investors, and other governments lose trust and look for other options for their money.

An example of this type of financial mismanagement occurred in Zimbabwe. In 2008, the inflation rate in Zimbabwe rose to over 79 billion percent—that's billion, with a "B".[13] Just like your airline points did in the previous example, people's life savings became worthless, as did their salaries. With no value left in their compensation, people stopped working, and schools and hospitals shut down. Zimbabweans didn't have a trustworthy currency in which to store the value they had acquired.

[13] Hanke S., & Kwok, A., "On the Measurement of Zimbabwe's Hyperinflation."

Citizens were seen pushing wheelbarrows full of cash to the market to buy food,[14] but even quadrillionaires could barely afford bread.[15]

. . . even quadrillionaires could barely afford bread

A similar situation occurred in 2018 in Venezuela, where inflation reached over 53 million percent.[16] If someone had invested $1 million in the Venezuelan Bolívar in 2013, they would have had less than 37 cents in 2019.[17] The average worker's daily wages were only enough to buy 900 calories of the cheapest food available.[18] People became desperate to find some way to store their earnings in a currency that would not inflate away to nothing. This led many people to turn to gold mining in hopes of securing monetary stability.

Think about gold as a store of value. No government owns or controls the global supply of gold, so there's no one single entity that can manipulate its price. Anyone can use gold to transact if they want to anywhere in the world. The challenge with gold is that it can be risky to store, cumbersome to transport, and most importantly, it can't be sent digitally. And so, while the older generations in Venezuela were trying to acquire gold, many younger, more tech-savvy Venezuelans began buying Bitcoin.

---

[14] Meldrum, "Where a basketful of groceries costs a bucketful of cash."

[15] Mushakavanhu, "I was a quadrillionaire in Zimbabwe, but could barely afford to buy bread."

[16] Cedrom, "BCV admite hiperinflación de 53.798.500% desde 2016."

[17] @RhythmTrader, Tweet.

[18] Vanek Smith, "The Measure Of A Tragedy."

Crypto Philanthropists

In December 2017, an individual using the pseudonym "Pine" announced the launch of the Pineapple Fund on Reddit.[19] The fund distributed a total of 5,057 bitcoins (~$55 million) to 60 charities.[20]

---

[19] u/PineappleFund, "I'm donating 5057 BTC to charitable causes! Introducing The Pineapple Fund."

[20] Partz, "Pineapple Fund Writes Farewell Post."

Bitcoin: Digital Gold

> *"Despite the government's attempts to be the sole issuers, there has been a constant flow of specialized currencies. In the early history of currency in Canada, every bank issued its own money."*
>
> - Ken Wyman, Consultant and Professor Emeritus of the Fundraising Management graduate program at Humber College

October 31, 2008 was the day that changed money forever. This was the day a mysterious person named "Satoshi Nakamoto" published a paper with a revolutionary new idea: Bitcoin.[21] Bitcoin was a new way to think about money, a system that didn't need governments to control it.

It was also a system that ensured that no more than 21 million bitcoins can ever be created, a programmed-in scarcity making it like a digital version of gold. Like gold, it doesn't have a central government managing it, and anyone can use it, anywhere in the world. What makes Bitcoin effective is that, unlike gold and traditional currencies, it is easy to send online. Today's financial system makes it very difficult and expensive to send money across borders. Services like bank wires or money transmitters like Western Union can take a long time and have fees that cost a significant percentage of the funds you're trying to send. With Bitcoin, someone can send a transaction to anyone else in the world in a matter of minutes for a relatively tiny fee. What's truly unique about this transaction is that there is no government or corporation mediating it. It is a direct peer-to-peer transaction.

You may be wondering how Bitcoin works if no government is controlling it. But, ask yourself this: who owns English? Who manages it and updates it? It is the users of English themselves that grow and evolve the language without a centralized control mechanism. Languages change because their

[21] Satoshi Nakamoto's identity remains unknown, though there has been much speculation, including the possibility that it could be a pseudonym for a group of people.

speakers come to a consensus on what new words mean. Bitcoin also operates on the concept of consensus—everyone agrees who owns the funds before the owner can send them.

Bitcoin is open source—anyone can view the code that is the backbone of the whole system.[22] The rules and parameters that govern its operations are transparently coded right in. For example, while fiat currency supply can be increased at the whim of a government, there will only ever be 21 million bitcoins produced, and they are released into the world in a structured fashion that everyone can see and understand. A group of coders called "Core Developers" maintain the Bitcoin code and implement any upgrades that are proposed and approved by the community.[23] If they are not implemented correctly, the community will reject the changes, and they will not be adopted.

What is Bitcoin Cash?

As you begin to accept cryptocurrency donations, you may see references to both "Bitcoin" and "Bitcoin Cash". It is important to know that these two cryptocurrencies are *not* the same; however, they have a shared history. The Bitcoin community disagreed on how to update the Bitcoin software to support the scaling of the cryptocurrency. As a result, the community decided to split into two separate blockchains and each pursued their own technical vision. This split is called a *hard fork*, and it created two different cryptocurrencies. This shared history can be compared to British English and American English. They both came from a common language, but have evolved independently and now have many elements that differentiate them.

[22] Bitcoin, "Bitcoin Core integration/staging tree."

[23] Bitcoin Core, "Bitcoin Development."

There are two key things to know about Bitcoin Cash. The first is that when people refer to "Bitcoin", they are never referring to Bitcoin Cash. The second is that, if you try to send Bitcoin to a Bitcoin Cash wallet, or vice versa, you will lose the funds. Be extra careful that you are sending the right cryptocurrency to the right type of wallet. The same applies to "Ether" and "Ether Classic".

There have been many attempts at digital money in the past, but Bitcoin is the first truly successful digital currency, in part because it solves the "double spend problem".

Bitcoin is the first truly successful digital currency, in part because it solves the "double spend problem"

Think back to an era where the internet didn't exist and information was only available in books. It was very difficult to share information widely, as nearly every person who wanted to read about a topic had to buy or borrow a copy of a particular book that was expensive to produce and cumbersome to distribute. Consequently, information was expensive, and books were only available to those with money. With the development of computers, information became digitized, and, with the advent of the internet, it became extremely easy to share. Just a few decades ago, if you had written an article and wanted to share it, you would have to physically publish the article—roughly one copy per reader. With the internet, the article could be published online and that single copy could be easily shared to millions of people, anywhere in the world.

The digitization of money offers similar promise—the ability to send money easily across the globe. But, unlike an article, you don't want the ability to take one unique dollar and send it to hundreds or thousands of people at the same time. This is called the "double spend problem": how to make money digital without enabling people to send the same dollar twice. For example, if someone had a digital dollar, you wouldn't want them to be able to donate that single dollar to your organization and to another organization at the same time, essentially copying and pasting to create two dollars when only one should exist. Bitcoin was able to solve this problem because it was built using an incredible new technology: the blockchain.

Crypto Philanthropists

An anonymous donor gave $280,000 to WikiLeaks in support of Julian Assange's defense fund in January 2021.[24]

[24] Smith, "Good Samaritan Donates $280,000 in Bitcoin to WikiLeaks Defence Fund."

Blockchain: The Foundation of Cryptocurrencies

> *"Every transaction that went out would actually detail where it was spent so anybody could go through and verify that their money was being spent correctly."*
>
> - Michael Tozoni, Treasurer of Bitcoin100

Throughout all of our daily digital activities, vast amounts of data are collected. Much of this data is stored in databases. Think of your donor database for example: all of the data about your donors is contained there, from their personal details to whether they opened the last e-newsletter. A blockchain is just a new way to store data. In this case, it's specifically storing data about transactions—like the section of your database that tells you the history of your donor's gifts. You can think about a blockchain as a digital record of transactions.

A blockchain is just a new way to store data

Imagine every single financial transaction that happens around the world every day. There are transactions between people, banks, corporations, and governments. Today, the records of those transactions are stored separately in the ledgers and accounts of each individual sender and recipient. For example, if a donation were made to your organization, that would show up as a credit in your accounts, and as a debit in the accounts of the donor. But what if, instead, all transactions made everywhere in the world were stored in one single record? That's how a blockchain works.

Each transaction of cryptocurrency is recorded and stored in groups with other transactions called blocks, and the blocks are connected in the format of a chain, hence the term blockchain.

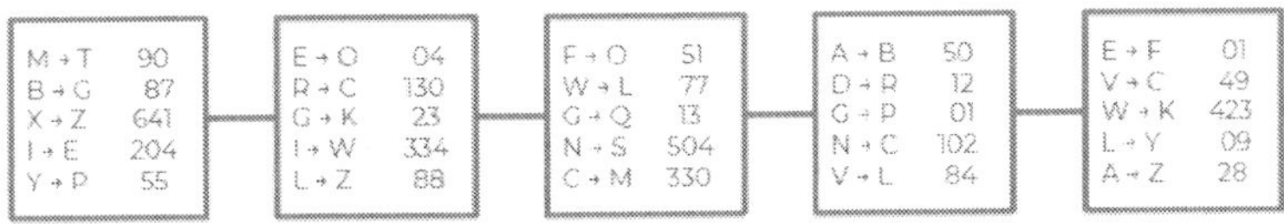

Each block is cryptographically linked to the block before it. It's a complex mechanism, but you can think about it as though each block has a photograph of the block before it coded right into it. If someone wanted to hack one of the transactions in a block, not only would they have to hack it in that block, but they would have to hack every single block that came after it, otherwise the picture wouldn't match. This property makes it extremely difficult, bordering on impossible, to hack.

There are many different blockchains out there—over 860 blockchains, in fact.[25] For example, Bitcoin and Ethereum are both blockchains, and each one has specific properties that make it more useful in particular use cases. Just like each country has its own fiat currency, each blockchain records the transactions of its own cryptocurrency. For the Bitcoin blockchain, the cryptocurrency is called Bitcoin; for the Ethereum blockchain, the cryptocurrency is called Ether. Blockchains can also log records like ownership certificates and other information.

There are four key properties of blockchains that are important to know:

Blockchains Are Decentralized

If the world only had one single ledger for all its transactions and that ledger was stored in one place, it would be easy to hack into, because the hacker would only need to do it once. To prevent this, a copy of the blockchain is stored on thousands of computers around the world. What makes it special is that it's truly accessible—anyone can download a copy of the software and the blockchain on their system. Even if someone were able to hack into

[25] BitDegree, "Did You Know There are 861 Blockchains?"

one transaction in one block, and then hack every single block that came after it, not only would they have to do it, but they would have to do it on thousands of computers at exactly the same time. But if everyone has a copy of the ledger, how do we know whose copy is right? The technical complexity of how this works is outside the scope of this book, but generally, the community comes to a consensus on who owned the money before it can be sent. This is much the same as English. When a new word is introduced, the community comes to a consensus about what that word means and how it is used.

Transactions Are Public to All Users

While some blockchain implementations are considered "private", such as a blockchain that's being used only amongst a group of banks, most of the donations you will receive will come from cryptocurrencies that use public blockchains. All transactions in a public blockchain, as with Bitcoin or Ethereum, are transparent and can be publicly accessed (more on this later).

Blockchains Are Immutable

The next key property of blockchains is that they are immutable, which means that once a transaction is made, it can't be edited or deleted. For example, once a gift is made, a donor cannot issue a chargeback like they could on a credit card, or change the value of the gift retroactively to make it smaller. All transactions are final.

Blockchains Are Power Resistant

The structure of a blockchain is such that powerful people or groups can't control them in the same way they might be able to control a corporation or a government. If your organization sent money to a vendor who then claimed they didn't receive it, not only could they not hide the transaction, edit the transaction, or delete the transaction, but they also couldn't work with a powerful person to shut off the blockchain to eliminate the ability to access the record itself.

Even the creator of a blockchain themselves cannot turn it off once it has been widely adopted. The record will always be available.

For these reasons, a blockchain is virtually unhackable. It's a single source of truth for everyone. It enables us to have the ease of peer-to-peer transactions like we used to in villages, but at a global scale, using cryptocurrencies. Blockchains provide the trust that centralized providers used to provide for us, and allow us to transact person-to-person in a new, global "village."

Crypto Philanthropists

In 2017, the Silicon Valley Community Foundation held approximately one third of its assets in cryptocurrency, amounting to approximately $4.5 billion.[26]

[26] PND, "Silicon Valley Community Foundation Held Billions in Digital Assets."

How to Buy Bitcoin

> *"It's clear to me that being prepared was half the battle. Being in a state of openness to get something of value is almost equally as valuable as putting it back out into the world."*
>
> - Jim Carter III, Founder of Cause Hack

One of the easiest ways to understand crypto donors and meaningfully connect with them is to become a member of the crypto community yourself. As a fundraiser, it's important for you to own cryptocurrency—even if it's only a nominal amount. First, you need to understand the process that your donors go through to buy, store, and sell their cryptocurrency. Donors will want to see that you are experienced in dealing with the asset so there won't be concerns of lost donations. Secondly, you will need to have gone through the process yourself, both to test your own donation process, and to effectively explain how it works to others on your team. And finally (and most importantly), some donors will want to see that you are part of the community, not just benefitting from it. You don't need to make an investment—buying just a very small amount of bitcoin will be enough to learn and test.

. . . some donors will want to see that you are part of the community, not just benefitting from it

---

Crypto Lingo

"Stacking Sats" ⟶ Short for "stacking satoshis", this phrase describes the practice of regularly buying and saving satoshis, the smallest fraction of a bitcoin. People who "stack sats" slowly buy satoshis to accumulate BTC over the long term.

Should you choose to take things a step further and personally invest in cryptoassets, remember this rule: never invest more than you are willing to lose.

The value of most cryptocurrencies is volatile. Experienced crypto owners are used to watching half the value of their investment disappear overnight. Most people aren't—and it's not a good feeling. If you invest in crypto, this **will** happen to you at some point. That's the downside of volatile markets. If you can't handle that stress, need your money to maintain its value because you need it in the short term, or are inexperienced in trading highly volatile assets, investing more than a few bucks in crypto is not for you.

Keeping Your Bitcoin Safe: Understanding Public and Private Keys

Bitcoin is built on something called asymmetric or public-key cryptography. This is a complex sounding term that can be simplified by thinking about your Bitcoin having two keys: a *public key*, that you can share, and a *private key*, that you keep secret.

If someone wants to send you a letter or a package in the mail, they can do so by using your home mailing address—this is information you can share publicly. By sharing your address with the sender, they can put the address on an envelope and drop it in the mail. Your address is information that is generally safe to share—any stranger can drop the item through your mail slot, but cannot actually enter your home and take any of your belongings.

Each cryptocurrency storage account (called a wallet) also has an address, called a public key or a public address. This public key can be sent to someone who wants to transfer Bitcoin to you; however, while they can send you funds with this information, they cannot access your wallet or remove any of the currency inside. A donor, for example, might request that you share your public key so they can transfer a donation from their wallet to the wallet belonging to your organization.

Unlike your house address, which is neatly organized into a house number, street name, and postal or zip code, a wallet's public address is a long string of letters and numbers. It might look something like this:

3GMSzFBrqqJhVS8gFEG5ThfAyZVU6jj1Dn

If you put the wrong address on a letter, it will not reach your recipient. The same applies if you misspell the public address by even one digit—when you send your Bitcoin, it will not reach your recipient. Any Bitcoin sent to the wrong address is gone forever and cannot be recovered.

To make sending your Bitcoin easier and less risky, many wallets will convert your public key into a QR code that can be scanned by the sender so there is no risk of typos or missing digits.

For example, here are both the public key and the QR code for the authors' wallet. After you get set up, feel free to test out making a transaction by scanning the QR code with your wallet and sending us some Bitcoin!

BTC Public Address:

3GMSzFBrqqJhVS8gFEG5ThfAyZVU6jj1Dn

BTC QR Code:

Your house also has a key to the front door, the *private key*. You keep that key safe and protected and generally don't share it with people who you don't know or can't trust—because practically speaking, the person holding that key can open your house and take all your stuff, regardless of whether they are legally allowed to do so.

Your wallet has a key that functions similarly to your house key. This is the private key mentioned above, and whoever has it can access, move, and spend the Bitcoin inside the wallet. A private key is made up of a long string of numbers and letters. This private key can also be represented as a "seed phrase" or "recovery phrase", which is a list of 12, 18, or 24 specific words in a specific order. It is critical that you write down and store your private key safely offline.

Security Alert

Never store your "seed phrase" or private key on any internet-connected device. When you are presented with a seed phrase, write it down and store it offline.

It is best to keep physical copies in separate locations to counter the risk of flood or fire damage in case of an emergency. The best way to think about security for your private key is to imagine it as a pile of cash. Would you leave a pile of cash in a desk drawer? Likely not. So don't leave your private key there. You might consider keeping a copy of your private keys in a safe deposit box. Private keys that are stored in a digital fashion, such as in your email or cloud drive, can be acquired by someone who has hacked your computer or online accounts. Your organization might choose to hold a copy of its private keys in an on-site safe and another at its bank. Your strategy will depend on how much crypto you are holding and moving.

Choosing a Wallet

To begin the process of buying and holding cryptocurrencies, you need to have a place to store your cryptocurrency. We call this a wallet. It's just like a wallet where you would store cash, except it's digital. There are many different types of wallets available and they range from apps on your phone for everyday transactions, to hardware wallets for long-term storage. If you choose to hold cryptocurrencies as a charitable organization, you will likely have a combination of wallets that you use for different purposes.

The first element to understand is the difference between a custodial and a non-custodial wallet.

Imagine you had a $100 bill. While legally, that money belongs to you, practically, the money belongs to whomever is holding that $100 bill. For example, if you drop that $100 bill in a park, and someone picks it up, that person can use the money to purchase anything. The holder of the bill has ownership over the money. The same is true of Bitcoin and other cryptocurrencies.

The person who holds the wallet's private key has ownership over the Bitcoin inside it and the ability to access it, send it, and spend it. The owner of the private key is the owner of the Bitcoin.

Crypto Lingo

"Not your keys, not your coins" ⟶ A phrase in the crypto community that describes the idea that if you don't hold your own private keys, your cryptocurrency no longer belongs to you.

Now imagine a scenario where you have $100 in the account of a company, like PayPal. You might consider that $100 more secure in PayPal because there's no physical bill that can fall out of your pocket in a park; however, you no longer have direct control over that money. If PayPal chooses to close your account or the company shuts down without warning, then because you no longer have access to your account or to your $100 bill, your money is lost.

The same principles apply to Bitcoin wallets. Custodial wallets are wallets where the company who made the wallet app controls and manages your private keys for you. On one hand, this can be useful because you can't lose your private key and subsequently lose access to your money. On the other hand, if the company that manages your wallet goes out of business or is prevented from operating, perhaps as a result of new government regulations, then you no longer have access to your money.

Security Alert

If you are using a "jailbroken" or "rooted" mobile phone, that means the manufacturer's default security protocols have been bypassed. It is not recommended that you conduct cryptocurrency transactions on such a device.

Most savvy cryptocurrency owners use non-custodial wallets, where they control their own private keys and subsequently maintain direct control over their money, like cash. There are numerous non-custodial wallets on the market, and those can be broken down into two main types that you may use as a part of your fundraising program: a hot wallet and a cold wallet.

Hot wallet → A hot wallet is a wallet that is directly connected to the internet. These wallets are typically accessible by mobile app or through a website. Because using internet-connected devices means potential risks from exposure to malware and system vulnerabilities, hot wallets should only be used to store smaller amounts of cryptocurrencies. You can download a hot wallet from your app store. Which wallet you choose will depend on your device (Apple vs. Android vs. web), your security needs, and the ease of use you require.

Cold wallet → A cold wallet is a wallet that is stored offline and subsequently less vulnerable to cyberattacks and hacking. The earliest form of cold wallet was a simple "paper wallet"—literally a piece of paper with your public and private keys written on it in various forms; these days they are considered cumbersome and obsolete, and are generally not recommended. Today, a cold wallet takes the form of a physical USB-like device called a hardware wallet, or hard wallet, that you can store in a fireproof safe or safe deposit box. You can order a hard wallet directly from the website of the company manufacturing them.

Security Tip

Never buy a hardware wallet secondhand or from anyone that isn't the original manufacturer, otherwise the seller may have accessed the private keys and could steal your funds.

Once you have a wallet set up, follow the directions to backup your account and safely store your private keys. Do not skip this step. Now you are ready to buy crypto!

Buying Cryptocurrencies

Before you start purchasing cryptocurrencies, be sure to track all of your purchases, sales, and trades including what you traded, at what rate, and on what date. This will be critical for reporting on your taxes. There is software on the market that will help you with this tracking, however we recommend keeping your own record in a spreadsheet as a backup.[27] Do not count on your exchange records to do this for you, as often exchanges will go under and your information will be lost.[28]

There are three main ways to purchase cryptocurrencies.

From another person ⟶ If you have a friend or family member who owns crypto, you can give them money directly and they can send you the crypto. There are also websites where anyone can connect directly with another person to buy and sell.[29]

A Bitcoin ATM (BTM) ⟶ Around the world, there are special ATMs that are purpose-built for Bitcoin transactions. Almost all of them will allow you to buy Bitcoin, and some also allow you to sell it. You can find current lists of where you can locate Bitcoin ATMs online. Bitcoin ATMs are often more expensive to use because they provide a level of anonymity that is not available through other purchase mechanisms.

An online exchange ⟶ Online exchanges are the most popular way to buy and sell cryptocurrencies. The same way you might exchange USD for Euros at a teller at the airport, someone can do the same with USD to

[27] Canadian Crypto.io, "Free Google Sheets Cryptocurrency Portfolio Tracker."
[28] Young, "75 crypto exchanges have closed down so far in 2020."
[29] Local Bitcoins, "LocalBitcoins."

Bitcoin, but do it online. You will need the type of exchange that has a way to get your fiat money into the cryptocurrency world. They do this by connecting to your bank account. Because they connect to the regular banking system, these exchanges are specific to a given country. Research the options in your country to see which exchange will be best for you. In the US and Canada, some exchanges have digital asset insurance in case of security breach or theft. Large borderless exchanges also exist: these allow you to trade one crypto for another, but they may not allow you to fund your account or withdraw funds unless the funds are in crypto format.

Security Tip: Never leave any cryptocurrency in your exchange account. After you complete your trade, always transfer your cryptocurrency out of the exchange and into your private wallet. If the exchange closes (which happens regularly), then your money is gone.

Exchanging Your Money

To buy Bitcoin for the first time, we recommend using an online exchange. As you go through this process, remember the first time you signed up for a bank account. It may have seemed easy at the time, but in retrospect, the process was likely quite intensive. You had to show up at a physical bank branch, during banker's hours, in the middle of a workday. You had to present a government-issued photo ID to a manager, and if the manager wasn't there, you had to come back another day. You filled out form after form—all on paper—and signed and dated them in duplicate copies. Getting set up to purchase crypto isn't all that different, it's just done online.

Exchanges must follow the same stringent regulations as banks to verify your identity and ensure that you aren't going to be performing illegal operations with the funds. As a result, the process of signing up for an online exchange can take days and sometimes even weeks depending on the capacity of the exchange to process applications. It is advised to sign up for multiple exchanges right away in case your preferred exchange takes a long time to approve your account or if it closes down without notice when you need to exchange your cryptocurrency.

To find the best exchange to use, google the exchanges for your country and ask people in the crypto community what exchanges they might recommend and why. Some exchanges may offer lower fees, others may have a better user interface that makes them easier for new users. You'll want to select an exchange that prioritizes the features you need most. Some exchanges only convert crypto to other crypto. Be sure to select an exchange that allows you to exchange your local currency for crypto and back again.

During your sign-up process, the exchange may ask you for information like a photo of your ID, a photo of yourself holding your ID, cell phone bills or other details that may seem a bit intrusive. Most exchanges don't want to collect your information—the Bitcoin community values privacy. These requests are made by exchanges in order to comply with governmental anti-money laundering laws, just like banks and other financial institutions do. Some exchanges will have varying levels of account verification. You can likely get started with a lower level of verification, however they may only permit larger transfers of funds to happen with the highest level of verification.

Most exchanages don't want to collect your information—the Bitcoin community values privacy

---

Once your account has been approved, you will want to ensure it is properly secured. This means enabling security features offered by the exchange, like two-factor authentication or "2FA".

Typically, when you log into an account on a website, if you have the username and the password, you can gain access. This makes it convenient to log in, but leaves you at risk if you have passwords auto-saved and someone steals your laptop or phone. 2FA means you need two methods of verification before it will let you access your account. The first is usually a username and password and the second is usually a text message code, an email verification, or most ideally, a security code from an authenticator application on your phone. Some donor databases have 2FA using a physical USB-like device that displays a six-digit number. An authenticator app is like a digital version of this device. Using two-step verification might be new and more cumbersome for you, but it is a critical step in protecting your account and any funds you have in it.

After you've completed setting up your security, you will need to connect your bank account to your profile to allow you to transfer money into the exchange. A small number of exchanges will allow you to do this with a credit card, however most will not. Typical options for transferring funds to exchanges include sending a wire transfer or sending an electronic funds transfer. There will be funding limits and differing fees for each of these methods. For example, many banks place an upper limit on the amount of funds that can be sent each day via an e-transfer. These same restrictions will apply here.

While some exchanges can automatically process e-transfers in as little as 30 minutes, it can take up to several days after you've sent your transfer for your funds to appear in your exchange account. Once this is complete, you are ready to trade your funds for cryptocurrencies.

Typically, exchanges that convert fiat to crypto (and vice versa) will offer a limited number of asset choices—these are commonly referred to as "tokens" and might include Bitcoin, Ether, and a few others. We will go into greater detail in the next section about the different categories of tokens available in the broader crypto ecosystem. If you have a donor who wants to contribute more unique tokens, you will have to find an exchange that accepts them and will convert your tokens into Bitcoin. These exchanges are typically large, global, and only accept crypto-to-crypto exchange. In other words, they don't have an interface with the traditional banking system—you need to already possess cryptocurrencies to buy, sell, and trade on them.

Decide on the token you want to purchase and use the "buy" functionality to trade your money for crypto. Congratulations—you are now the proud owner of cryptocurrencies and a member of the crypto community!

Crypto History

Mt Gox (pronounced "Mount Gox") was one of the world's first cryptocurrency exchanges.[30] Based in Japan, Mt Gox launched in 2010, and began accepting wire transfers from all over the world from users looking to trade their fiat currencies for crypto. In 2014, the exchange abruptly halted trading and went offline, leaving customers without access to their accounts and any money held within them. It was later discovered that over 744,000 bitcoin had been stolen. At one point creditors were owed over $2.4 trillion, most of which has never been paid back.[31, 32]

[30] Wikipedia, "Mt. Gox."

[31] Rizzo, "Mt. Gox Allegedly Loses $350 Million in Bitcoin."

[32] Mt. Gox, "Mt Gox Announcement of February 17th, 2014."

Quadriga CX was one of the longest-running exchanges in the Canadian market. In 2018, founder and CEO Gerald Cotten died unexpectedly while traveling in India. He had sole control over the cold wallets where the user funds were being held.[33] Over 76,000 customers lost access to any funds they had in their exchange accounts, totalling over $214 million.[34]

Once you have traded your money for cryptocurrency, you should transfer it out into your wallet. To do this, you will use the exchange's withdraw function. You will need to copy and paste your wallet address into the exchange to withdraw the funds. Be sure that if you are sending bitcoin, that you send it to a Bitcoin wallet address and not a Bitcoin Cash wallet address (see the pop-out box in the section Bitcoin: Digital Gold for more on this).

The transaction shouldn't take more than a few minutes. If the crypto hasn't arrived in your wallet, you can use a block explorer to verify if the transaction has gone through and see where the money is (we cover this in the next section, How to Donate Bitcoin). While transfers of cryptocurrencies will typically only take a few minutes, if you have sold crypto to get your local currency back via the exchange, it may take much longer to get your funds. The exchange will have to transfer the funds via their bank to your bank, which can take several days to execute.

---

[33] Copeland, "The complete story of the QuadrigaCX $190 million scandal."

[34] Doucette, "Tales from the crypto: Clients want to see human remains of QuadrigaCX founder."

Security Tip

Always send a test transaction (a tiny amount of cryptocurrency) before sending large amounts of money to be sure you have entered in the wallet address correctly. If you make a mistake, the funds are lost and cannot be returned.

It is absolutely critical that you do not leave funds in your exchange account. Most exchanges are centralized private companies that are vulnerable to the same attacks as any other company, including data theft, hackers stealing funds, employees stealing funds, or even the accidental loss of funds or bankruptcy due to mismanagement. There have been numerous examples of cryptocurrency exchanges that have gone under, taking their customers' funds with them. Do not let this happen to you—always immediately transfer your funds into a wallet or your bank account.

Crypto Philanthropists

Justin Sun, the founder of the Tron blockchain, donated $1 million to Greta Thunberg's climate work. He previously donated $4.6 million to the Glide Foundation.[35]

[35] The Giving Block, "What is #BagSeason?"

How to Donate Bitcoin

> *"Within 8 weeks of setting up cryptocurrency donations, we received $42,000 in donations from event sponsorships and COVID relief initiatives."*
>
> - Henah Parikh, Development and Communications Manager at She's the First

A cryptocurrency donation is essentially just one person sending cryptocurrency to another—in this case, a donor sending crypto to your organization. When you think about having to send money across the world to another person, it's a daunting task. You either have to physically go to a bank branch to send a wire, which can take a week to arrive and often comes with expensive fees, or use a company like Western Union or MoneyGram to send your funds. These operators often charge transaction fees in addition to their exchange rates and the process can take several days. Digital options like PayPal are easier, but still cost charities a percentage-based fee to receive a donation. They also run the risk of removing access to your account, subsequently locking you out of your money.[36] Sending Bitcoin or another cryptocurrency from one person to another is comparatively cheaper, faster, and more secure.

A cryptocurrency donation is essentially just one person sending cryptocurrency to another

---

In order for someone to donate Bitcoin to your organization, your charity would need to provide the donor with a copy of its public key. This might be directly posted on your website, either in raw format or as a QR code, or

[36] King, "Frozen Paypal account a nightmare for unemployed man."

might be provided only to donors once they have connected with your team and are ready to make a donation. The donor will then go to the "send" function of their wallet, scan the QR code or enter in the public key, enter in the amount, and hit send.

Security Tip

To avoid issues when sending cryptocurrencies, always choose to scan the QR code instead of typing in a public address. Once the address appears in your wallet's send function, double check that it matches the address you want to send it to.

The transaction will take about 10 minutes to be confirmed. This process is undertaken so that it can be verified that the sender of the funds actually owned the funds and wasn't trying to spend them twice. You will see the transaction in your wallet, perhaps with a note saying the number of confirmations that have been achieved. Each confirmation further strengthens the transaction against fraud. Typically it is recommended to wait for six confirmations before considering a transaction fully verified. This can take up to an hour. If, for some reason, the donor claims to have sent the funds, but the organization is not seeing the funds in their wallet, you can use a website called a block explorer to see what happened with the transaction.

Each transaction made on a blockchain is tracked in a transparent manner. For public blockchains like Bitcoin and Ethereum, the transactions and their details are public. These transactions can be viewed using a block explorer. Each blockchain will have many block explorer sites where you can access the same information. Because each cryptocurrency has its own blockchain, if you search an Ethereum transaction on a Bitcoin block explorer, you will not find anything.

Each transaction has a transaction number called a hash. This looks like a really long string of letters and numbers and is essentially just a way to uniquely identify the transaction, the same way each donor in your donor file would have their own unique identifier. The picture below shows what that looks like.[37]

Hash	Time	Amount (BTC)	Amount (USD)
f8ec92785aac2bace9156d786a625668c3e113a50ccf4bdb535d175219a5f486	16:46	0.01689709 BTC	$155.97
e3fdf2b36a8c25e174253fbdd301539332d58a8c0ff5950f24cb916e2c343660	16:46	0.55332929 BTC	$5,107.51
82d6756a77364b30df0d806de33ce09d5445b75b7e2346a4225c20f43d37465a	16:46	15.38225829 BTC	$141,985.94
b8bbe82f6a6eaa3e3bc6e2c263ac9080a7cb45bf33b6a4ecdab92380c8fdad10	16:46	0.00284152 BTC	$26.23
7723cda6aceaa1b823554d492fc41ed83aacbd78cbf272ab9b899f3238a64606	16:46	0.04236405 BTC	$391.04
d1f2a4390e1de5263d06f5171934d9a03323581b1f0b5c5f30785bf09e1275ef	16:46	0.00853149 BTC	$78.75
8f61d9f9a1dd7a2b3af6cdf5d623d3d956a5f8ec649bf97b20c2e6ebf9286fe7	16:46	0.05192084 BTC	$479.26
377418991f01e706ee96d0427e44a13ec59f6c9de2ab743687efaaf1c1cba8a9	16:46	0.04254062 BTC	$392.67

Each hash contains information about the transaction. When you click on the hash of one particular transaction, it will lead you to the details you see below. On the left, you have the address the transaction came from, and on the right, the addresses where the funds went. On the far right, you can see how much Bitcoin was sent.[38]

As you can see, the addresses themselves don't provide any identifying information as to the sender or the receiver. In this sense, public blockchain transactions are both completely traceable and anonymous at the same time. Many consider Bitcoin to be "pseudonymous" as a result.

[37] Blockchain.com, "Bitcoin Explorer."
[38] Blockchain.com, "Transaction Summary."

You can ask the donor to send you the hash of the transaction and then verify that the address they sent it to belongs to the organization. You can also search your organization's public address and see which transactions were sent to it. If the block explorer is showing that your wallet address was correct and that it received the funds, but they aren't showing up in your wallet, try waiting another hour or two. Otherwise, contact your wallet provider to help troubleshoot. The worst case scenario is that you take your private key—that you stored during the backup—and upload it to another wallet and all of the funds will be there. If the transaction details show that the donor either didn't send the money at all, or sent it to the wrong address, then the organization never received the money and the donor has lost the funds and will not be able to get them back. For this reason, it is critical for larger gifts to have the donor do a test transaction to ensure they have the correct details. In the case of a donation made through a giving platform that processes crypto donations, this won't be an issue for your organization, as the platform will be responsible for tracing that.

Crypto Philanthropists

Gemini, the crypto exchange owned by Tyler and Cameron Winklevoss, donated $50,000 to the Human Rights Foundation in December 2020. [39]

[39] Harper, "Gemini Donates $50K to HRF."

Types of Tokens

"I was excited to support a charity that exists, survives, and flourishes based on the crypto space and cryptocurrencies as donations."

- Andrew, Crypto Donor and Investor

There are many different financial instruments available that donors can use to donate wealth to a nonprofit. For example, a donor could make a gift of cash, real estate, or securities. "Securities" is a term that describes a class of financial instruments that represent either ownership of shares (stock) or ownership of debt (bonds) in a company. The term "cryptoasset" is similar in that it is an umbrella term that encompasses a variety of token types that all fall under one asset class. Understanding the different types of cryptoassets can help you, as a fundraiser, to understand the philosophy behind why a donor might have purchased that type of token, and to tailor your ask to better match their personal ethos. There are four main categories of cryptoassets: cryptocurrencies, utility tokens, security tokens, and non-fungible tokens.

Understanding the different types of cryptoassets can help you understand the philosophy of your donor

---

Cryptocurrencies/Coins

While the term cryptocurrency is often used as an umbrella term to describe most virtual currencies that are decentralized in nature, it specifically refers to digital currencies that have their own blockchains. You can think about cryptocurrencies like money. Examples include Bitcoin, abbreviated to BTC (of the Bitcoin blockchain), and Ether, abbreviated to ETH (of the

Ethereum blockchain). These types of cryptoassets are the most widely owned and the ones you will see most often in your fundraising programs.

Crypto Lingo

'Altcoin' ⟶ Short for "alternative coin", the term altcoin refers to any cryptocurrency, token, or cryptoasset that isn't Bitcoin.

Utility Tokens

Utility tokens are cryptoassets that enable you to use a product or perform a function in an application. You can compare it to buying cell phone credits to access a mobile network: the credits enable you to utilize the network to make calls. You can also think of them like arcade tokens that allow you to play the games. For example, a developer might build an application to track a soybean supply chain. The app could be built using the Ethereum blockchain as a base and would make certain payments in Ether to run the app. However, users of the app would also need to purchase "Soycoin" tokens to use the app itself. Thus, the token provides you with the 'utility' of using the app. Examples of utility tokens include BAT, the Brave browser's "Basic Attention Token", and Storj, the token for the distributed cloud storage company of the same name.

Initial Coin Offerings

An initial coin offering (ICO) is a crowdfunding mechanism by which crypto companies offer tokens for sale to the general public to raise money to build out their vision, like if an arcade sold their game tokens in advance to raise money to build the arcade itself. You may also hear them referred to as TGE (Token Generation Events). This is similar to how an ordinary company would do an IPO (Initial Public Offering) and sell their shares on a stock market. The benefit of an ICO is that it can help fund projects that couldn't be easily funded through traditional channels. If you have a great concept for infrastructure technology, and if the community members believe in your vision and the value your project will bring to the community, they will buy the tokens and support the project's creation.

While the first ICO occurred in 2013,[40] it wasn't until 2017 that they really took off, when nearly every crypto company was creating a token and selling it to investors, often making millions of dollars in a matter of hours. This led to the creation of a lot of tokens that didn't really add value to projects or to the community. There was a massive spike in the market—and then the bubble popped and prices crashed. As a result, new token launches are met today with more skepticism and discernment than they were historically. In addition, securities regulators have stepped in with compliance requirements to prevent fraud. Nevertheless, ICOs still remain an effective new business model to fund large-scale projects.

Security Tokens

Security tokens differ from the other types in that, instead of having inherent value, they are a representation of an investment. While there are many complex applications, we'll share two key examples here. The first is an investment in a company. In the same way that a person can buy shares in a company today, blockchain companies have started issuing tokens that represent ownership of the company instead of shares.[41] The second is an

[40] Wikipedia, "Initial Coin Offering."

[41] Stoner, "Polymath Launches 'Token Studio 2.0' on 'Polymesh' Digital Securities Blockchain."

investment in real estate. Imagine you'd like to invest in a large apartment complex in New York City. To do so would be expensive and inaccessible to most individuals. Blockchain companies are now "tokenizing" buildings—in other words, splitting the ownership of a building (and its value) into tokens.[42] Investors can buy as little as a single token, say for $1, and sell it whenever they want. It is unlikely you will see any security tokens as a part of your fundraising in the short term; however, they will likely become more prevalent in the future.

Non-Fungible Tokens (NFT)

When holding a cryptocurrency like Bitcoin or Ether, just like when you have a dollar, whether you have one coin or another coin of the same denomination is irrelevant—they are all the same. Non-Fungible Tokens, or NFTs, provide a way to represent and confirm the uniqueness of digital goods. The holder of an NFT would have verifiable ownership of a digital good that was unlike any other. An example of an application of an NFT is CryptoKitties, a platform in which users can buy and exchange virtual cats. Each unique virtual cat is represented by an NFT and can be easily transferred to anyone else on the Ethereum blockchain. Another example is SuperRare, a platform which uses NFTs to verify and authenticate unique digital artworks. Both CryptoKitties and SuperRare have held auctions for NFTs that have raised hundreds of thousands of dollars for charities. Just as nonprofits may occasionally see donations of high value in-kind goods, they may encounter donors who own and may wish to donate NFTs.

Within these categories you will find further subcategories of cryptoassets that often describe the function of a token or coin. This function makes the asset unique in a particular way, and a differentiating factor that may lead a particular type of donor to own it, use it, or donate it.

---

[42] De, "$66 Million Building to Be Tokenized on Ethereum Blockchain in Record Deal."

Stablecoins

Looking at historical price charts, it's easy to see that cryptoassets are highly volatile. For many of these assets, it wasn't unusual to see one drop 40% of its value in a matter of days, and then rise 500% the following month. This created challenges for people who couldn't handle that level of volatility for their needs. This led to the creation of "stablecoins" or "stable tokens," crypto assets that are designed to minimize volatility. Typically this is done by assigning them the same value as, or "pegging" them to, either a single fiat currency, like the US Dollar, Euro, or Yen, or an average value made from a basket of currencies. Others are pegged to gold or other cryptocurrencies. This allows users to accurately predict the price and avoid volatility. Additional practices like providing verifiable proof of reserves help to offer additional stability. Examples of stablecoins include DAI, USD Coin (USDC), and Tether (USDT).

Privacy Coins

While it may seem that Bitcoin transactions are anonymous, they are actually traceable to a certain degree. There are, as a result, cryptocurrencies that are built to provide significantly higher levels of privacy for users, so their transactions can't be traced at all. Examples of privacy coins include Monero, Dash, and Zcash. At the time of writing, there are considerations by some exchanges to delist these coins due to changing compliance requirements that have been set by local regulators.

It will be up to you and your team to determine which cryptocurrencies or tokens you will accept as a part of your donation program. Depending on the type of setup you choose, accepting more types of cryptoassets may bring in a greater number of donors; however, it may also add significant complexity and additional work to the management of the program. Some tokens will require additional wallet types or signing up for additional exchanges.

You may want to start with a smaller number of assets and increase your acceptance as your team becomes more comfortable with the process.

Crypto Philanthropists

In 2018, an anonymous donor gave $5 million in Bitcoin to the California-based Open Medicine Foundation.[43]

Learn the Basics Checklist

- ❑ Research the legal and tax regulations regarding cryptocurrencies in your country
- ❑ Download and set up a wallet for yourself
- ❑ Make a backup copy of your wallet's private keys
- ❑ Sign up for a personal exchange account
- ❑ Transfer funds from your bank to your exchange
- ❑ Buy Bitcoin or another cryptoasset on the exchange
- ❑ Transfer the crypto out of the exchange and into your wallet
- ❑ Track your crypto purchases to have a record for your taxes
- ❑ Practice making a transaction, sending crypto to a friend, or donating to a charity that accepts crypto already

[43] Kelly, "Anonymous bitcoin philanthropist donates $5 million."

II: Set Up Your Program

Getting Started

> *"It's an odd idea that [donors] would start by saying, 'I'm just looking for a charity that will accept this' rather than being mission driven or responding to an appeal. "*
>
> - Ken Wyman, Consultant and Professor Emeritus of the Fundraising Management graduate program at Humber College

Over the years, we have set up, guided, and advised successful cryptocurrency programs at numerous nonprofit organizations. With each passing year, the technical complexities of setting up a cryptocurrency program grow simpler, while other things, like securing internal organizational support, remain consistently challenging.

These difficulties are not unique to cryptocurrency donation programs. Clearly articulating and communicating the benefits of a new program can be a lot of work, but doing so is important in order to move forward.

The sections ahead will help guide you through the various steps in setting up a program in the context of a nonprofit organization and help you to address some of the questions, concerns, and challenges that may arise.

As you are getting started, reach out to others in the nonprofit and cryptocurrency communities for support. You may be surprised at the knowledge that exists in your extended networks if you share on social media that you are looking at setting up a program.

As you set up your program, you will join a global network of nonprofit innovators who are preparing their organizations for the future. Networks function better with more participants and, as the proverb goes, "if you want to go fast, go alone; if you want to go far, go together." As nonprofit cryptocurrency communities continue to grow, we encourage you to share your knowledge to help others who may benefit from your experience.

Securing Organizational Support

> *"[Fundraisers] are often surprised to hear people have donated hundreds of millions of dollars in crypto."*
>
> - Alex Wilson, CEO and Co-Founder of The Giving Block

The single most important factor that will determine the success of a cryptocurrency implementation is organizational support. This consideration is not solely limited to cryptocurrency programs; having the support of key stakeholders when launching any project helps ensure a higher likelihood of success. It's a lot easier to get stuff done when people have bought in to your vision.

Educating individuals on the benefits is an important step that must be taken when championing a potential new cryptocurrency donation program. While organizations may differ in terms of context, size, scope, mission, and capacity, there are many common themes that will be helpful to secure organizational support.

Key Drivers for Adoption

Identifying and recognizing key drivers for adoption will help answer the question of *why* a cryptocurrency program may be beneficial for your organization and help you to frame your approach. Common key drivers that may apply to your organization include:

1) **The need to raise additional funds**

   Fundraising is often a primary consideration for many organizations in order to ensure mission delivery, and a cryptocurrency program offers an opportunity to diversify revenue streams and increase donations.

2) **The desire to engage new donor audiences**

   Often when new fundraising initiatives are launched, there are concerns that they may compete with other campaigns and make asks of the same donors already on file. The most successful new fundraising activities are ones that are strategic and take into consideration the full donor journey, in addition to bringing in new segments of donors. As existing donor bases continue to mature and change, cryptocurrencies can play a part in revitalizing a donor file without taking funds from other activities.

3) **The need to innovate**

   Organizations may be pressed by their boards and senior management to demonstrate innovation. Unlike other activities, a cryptocurrency implementation may offer a well-defined project with a financial return as a component of a broader innovation strategy.

4) **Preparing for the future**

   The rapid and enduring growth of cryptocurrency and its adoption by major corporations like Microsoft, Facebook, and PayPal, along with acknowledgement by banking regulators, have validated the technology.[44] Organizations are recognizing the need to adapt. Cryptocurrencies continue to influence various areas, with government policy evolving to take into consideration a changing landscape and financial institutions evaluating their investment portfolios. Organizations that wish to be well-prepared for the future can implement a cryptocurrency program, allowing them to respond quickly to donors who wish to make

[44] Gould, "OCC Chief Counsel's Interpretation."

gifts in cryptocurrency, rather than scrambling to set up a program when the request is made.

Assessing Organizational Capacity and Adoption

When considering a cryptocurrency donation program, you will need to assess your organization's capacity to adopt technology to better serve its mission.[45] If a good predictor of future behaviour is past behaviour, understanding your organization's previous successes and failures with innovation and technology initiatives will help you identify where you may need to focus your efforts in order to move a cryptocurrency donation program forward.

While every organization differs in its capacity and comfort level with regards to change and technology adoption, considering a cryptocurrency program is not a matter of *if* you should move ahead, but a strategic decision of *when* and *how* you will incorporate cryptocurrencies. An organization generally doesn't question whether or not it is going to be using the internet; the strategic question is *how* they will use it to advance their mission. Similarly, cryptocurrency is not an *if*, but a *when*.

[it's] not a matter of if you should move ahead, but a strategic decision of when and how you will incorporate cryptocurrencies

---

In *Diffusion of Innovations*, Everett Rogers outlines how innovations are adopted among organizations and provides a model that can be used for understanding how cryptocurrency uptake is unfolding among nonprofits.

[45] If you are looking to measure your tech practices, NTEN offers a free benchmarking assessment of organizational use and policies around technology: https://www.nten.org/accelerate/.

The diagram below outlines this model with regards to the various stages and adopters. At what stage has your organization typically adopted other technologies or innovations? This will give you a rough idea of where your organization is situated, and the types of conversations you will likely need to have and the time required to get a project rolling.

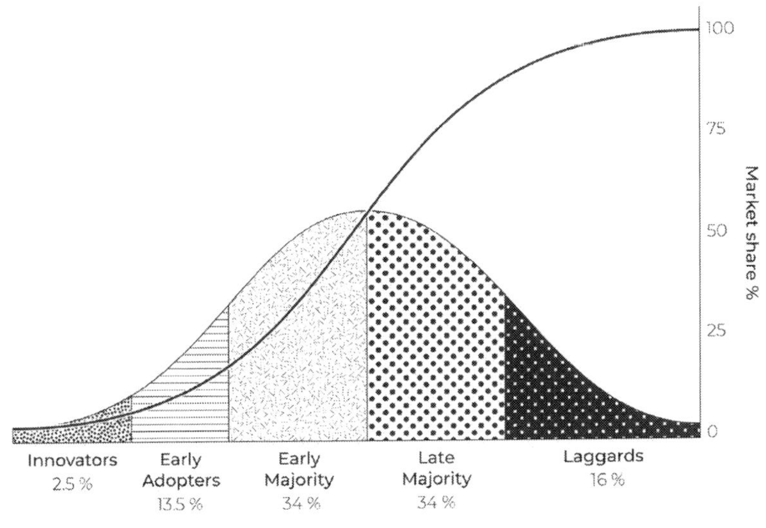

Diffusion of Innovations [46]

The amount of time that you may need to spend educating individuals on the value of innovation and potential benefits of a cryptocurrency donation program will vary. If your organization tends to adopt technology and innovation at earlier stages, you can likely get started right away. If your organization is typically closer to the right of the adoption curve, be prepared to examine and address underlying barriers to adoption. If this is the case, you may want to start the conversation as soon as possible to begin

---

[46] Wikimedia, "Diffusion of Ideas."

the process of making people comfortable with the idea of accepting cryptocurrencies. However, one thing is certain: even the most forward-thinking nonprofits require clear communication and organizational support to move ahead with new initiatives.

Alignment With Your Organization's Mission and Values

The implementation of a cryptocurrency donation program may offer additional opportunities for your organization to live out its mission, vision, and values. The beliefs that have shaped the development of cryptocurrency may be particularly well-aligned if your organization's mission and/or vision includes the advancement of privacy, poverty reduction, access to financial services, free speech, liberty, innovation, or technology.

Many nonprofit organizations also articulate a set of values that guide how the organization's mission is accomplished. If your organization has a clear set of values that are being measured and evaluated as part of an annual performance review process, a cryptocurrency implementation may be a good fit, especially if those values include innovation, adaptability, learning, or creativity.

Understanding Strategic Priorities

Alignment with strategic priorities is a key factor in securing support for a new concept. Each organization differs in how these priorities are documented, but they can often be found within a strategic plan or the documentation generated from an annual planning process.

If your organization's strategic priorities include raising additional funds, diversifying revenue streams, engaging new donor audiences, or advancing innovation, a cryptocurrency program may be well-aligned and regarded as a natural extension of existing work. After all, it's simpler to find ways that a cryptocurrency project can support your organization's priorities than it will be to revamp the strategic plan.

For organizations that have longer-term strategic plans in place, this may provide an opportunity to situate a cryptocurrency implementation as a multi-year endeavour, starting with a simple implementation to accept Bitcoin. Subsequent years may include the consideration of other cryptocurrencies and tokens, partnerships, or advanced implementations.

Taking the time to evaluate and assess potential alignments with strategic priorities will ensure that you can justify and secure the time and resources required. If the objectives of a cryptocurrency program are fundamentally misaligned with your organization's strategic priorities, it will be difficult for others to see the value in it.

Securing Executive Support

Executive support plays a critical role in determining the success of a cryptocurrency donation program. When preparing a case for executive support, start with considering senior management and addressing your organization's key strategic concerns. Provide clarity around what is needed to carry out an implementation and its expected benefits. What are the most pressing concerns of the executive leadership in your organization? Understanding the answer to this question will help clarify what you should focus on. Above all else, when preparing to secure executive support for a cryptocurrency program, ensure that you know your audience.

In knowing your executive audience, consider the things that they are responsible for and how a cryptocurrency project may be helpful. For example, if you are securing support from someone whose responsibilities include revenue generation, they may be more interested in cryptocurrency's potential for fundraising rather than the technology itself. On the broad range of key strategic concerns for organizations, unless your nonprofit is focused on the crypto space, cryptocurrency may not be the first thing that comes to mind for senior leaders. You will have to determine what may be of interest to your audiences. When addressing senior management, consider questions that have typically been raised when previous projects have been proposed. In our experience, the concerns that are raised most often by senior management typically focus on staffing resources, costs, and security.

Knowing your audience also means understanding precisely what you are pitching. Are you informing them about a new cryptocurrency project or asking for their approval? A common misstep is asking for permission to do your job. If your job entails raising more revenue, or advancing innovation, focus on highlighting the benefits to the organization and what is needed to move it ahead. Ask for support, not permission.

While executive support can take the form of direct support from an Executive Director, CEO, or another senior staff member of your organization, it can also come from the board.[47] Securing this support ensures that you have a mandate to move ahead and secure resources to set up and sustain a program.

Ask for support, not permission

We are often asked by nonprofit staff about how to approach boards when exploring the use and acceptance of cryptocurrencies. It is helpful to draw a distinction between seeking permission and securing support, especially at the board level. Governance boards should generally be concerned with broad strategy and direction for an organization, and a crypto donation program would typically be classified as an operational consideration. An exception may apply if you operate with a working (or operational) board; in that case, your board may be very hands-on. A litmus test for your organization may be that if you typically wouldn't ask your board for

[47] If you are reading this as an executive leader, while you may be able to issue a directive to move ahead, this section may be helpful in communicating the details to your peers and direct reports.

approval on the finer details of your fundraising operations, such as accepting credit cards on your website or setting up in-kind gifts of securities, you likely don't need to seek board approval to accept cryptocurrencies. However, the implementation of a cryptocurrency program may be a welcome update at a board meeting and it will be helpful to ensure that you are prepared for any questions that may arise. In addition, provide resources for board members to share so that they can advocate for and champion your program once it is implemented.

A Cryptocurrency Working Group

In some cases, it may be possible to single-handedly implement a cryptocurrency donation program within your organization, but often there will be benefits to approaching this with a working group or internal committee. When thoughtfully assembled, a working group can be effective in bringing the right people together to secure support from the bottom up. Approaching senior executives or board members will be easier if all the key parties on the operational side are already on board.

A Cryptocurrency Working Group should ideally consider the inclusion of both the Head of Finance and Head of Fundraising in your organization, as there are often questions that need to be addressed from both a finance and a fundraising perspective. When considering staff members for the working group, think about inviting individuals whose work will be directly impacted by an implementation, as well as those whose lack of support and buy-in could halt or delay the project. These voices are needed to ensure that everyone is on board. This process of co-creation can be valuable, as new operational methods that are developed at the highest level can be blocked in practice by frontline staff who may refuse to take action on ideas they had no voice in deciding. It will also help ensure that you have additional people to support your endeavour and advocate for it to the various parts of your organization. The working group will provide multiple perspectives to propose supporting policies and frameworks.

A "terms of reference" document may be helpful in providing clarity for working group members when getting started. Below is a basic sample that may be modified for your own purposes:

Cryptocurrency Working Group Terms of Reference

Date of last revision:

Approved by:

Date Approved:

Purpose:

The purpose of the Cryptocurrency Working Group is to develop and implement a cryptocurrency donation program.

Responsibilities and Scope:

The Cryptocurrency Working Group's scope of activities includes:

- Implementation of a cryptocurrency donation program
- Establishing timelines for implementation
- Proposing policies and frameworks needed to support a cryptocurrency donation program
- Educating staff on the basics of cryptocurrency
- Identification and implementation of best practices
- Sharing progress and highlighting success stories

Membership:

Members of the Cryptocurrency Working Group shall include representation from the fundraising and finance departments. In addition, members may include stakeholders whose work is directly impacted by a cryptocurrency program implementation. The Chair of the group shall be determined by the members of the Working Group.

Frequency of Meetings:

The Cryptocurrency Working Group shall meet at such times as determined by the Chair. The Cryptocurrency Working Group will continue to meet until the work is completed or the Working Group members decide to disband.

An additional document that may also be helpful to the Cryptocurrency Working Group is a briefing note on cryptocurrency donations. A briefing note provides an overview about the project that can serve to inform others who are looking to quickly get up to speed, and can also serve as a handy reference.

For a briefing note, here are some points that may be helpful to cover:

- Executive Summary
- What is Bitcoin and why is it relevant to our organization?
- How does this align with our organization's mission, vision, and/or strategy?
- What is the opportunity?
- What are the risks?
- What is the cost?
- What would an implementation look like?
- Next Steps

Sample Briefing Note

Bitcoin Briefing Note

Executive Summary

Bitcoin is a cryptocurrency that has been adopted around the world. There is an opportunity for our organization to connect with a whole new community of donors, and accept donations of cryptocurrencies to support our mission.

What is Bitcoin and why is it relevant to our organization?

Bitcoin is a cryptocurrency that was invented in 2008 and has rapidly gained adoption and legitimacy worldwide. A single Bitcoin that was valued at less than a cent in 2010 is now worth over $40,000 (in January 2021).[48, 49] For some investors, this has resulted in significant gains of wealth, which presents an opportunity for our organization to accept Bitcoin and develop plans to identify and build relationships with those who may be interested in supporting our mission via cryptocurrency.

How does this align with our strategy?

Raising additional revenue, increasing awareness, and advancing innovation have been identified as strategic priorities for our organization to advance its mission. A cryptocurrency project will directly speak to these priorities:

1) *Raising additional revenue* - Providing a new channel of donations as well as opportunities to engage with those involved with cryptocurrencies.

---

[48] Bitcoin Pizza Index, "Bitcoin Pizza Index."

[49] Coinmarketcap, "Coinmarketcap."

2) *Increasing awareness* - Providing additional opportunities to highlight the project to the media and focused outreach to tech-savvy audiences.
3) *Advancing innovation* - As payment ecosystems and technology continue to evolve, this provides an opportunity for us to explore how Bitcoin and related technologies can benefit the work that we do so that we are prepared for the future. This will also aid in positioning our organization as an innovative leader to donors and partners.

What is the opportunity?

There have been a number of major gifts that have been made by crypto-philanthropists, including Vitalik Buterin ($2.4 million to SENS Research Foundation) and the Pineapple Fund ($55 million to 60 charities). In addition, Fidelity Charitable has received over $100 million in donations of cryptocurrency since 2015. Currently, if a donor wishes to make a gift of cryptocurrency, we are not capable of accepting it—that is the opportunity.

Accepting Bitcoin donations will allow our organization to raise additional funds and further diversify our revenue streams. As digital currencies continue to mature, our adoption of cryptocurrencies will ensure that we will be well-prepared for other benefits they might bring to our operations.

What are the risks?

One distinct possibility is that few donations will be received, particularly in the early stages of the program. Like any new fundraising channel, it will take time to grow. There are often perceived risks related to the price volatility of Bitcoin, but this can be mitigated by immediately liquidating the cryptocurrency upon receipt to secure its value.

What is the cost?

The costs of accepting cryptocurrencies are limited to staff time for implementation and the fees for usage of a platform. Platform fees are typically embedded in the cost of each individual transaction and are typically no more than 1-2%.

What would an implementation look like?

A cryptocurrency donation program is relatively simple to implement and the initial steps will involve identifying a payment processor that can be embedded on our website. From there, donors may be directed to our website to make donations in cryptocurrency, just like traditional donors will go online to donate by credit card. Over time, marketing and promotion will be helpful to support ongoing awareness.

Next Steps

Confirm members for a cryptocurrency working group and proceed with implementation.

Crypto Philanthropists

In 2019, stablecoin producer Tether pledged $10 million to Deltec Cares, a local organization in the Bahamas, to support victims following hurricane Dorian.[50]

[50] Ogwu, "Tether donates $1 million to help victims in hurricane Dorian-ravaged Bahamas."

Making the Case for a Cryptocurrency Donation Program

> *"The acceptance of cryptocurrency is an important trend in the future. The really important discussion is what holds charities back from adopting new methods, because this is such a widespread problem."*
>
> - Ken Wyman, Consultant and Professor Emeritus of the Fundraising Management graduate program at Humber College

Just like in fundraising, a powerful way to illustrate the opportunity for your organizational leadership is to use storytelling. What will your organization look like in the future? What would additional funding from a cryptocurrency program enable? How could your programs change or grow if there were new donors supporting your mission? The vision that you share and rally support around may be an organization that looks ahead and adopts technology to meet its mission. Beyond implementing a cryptocurrency donation program, you are also helping to paint a picture of what is possible because of it.

As an innovative leader working toward a cryptocurrency donation program at your organization, remember the need to set the tone. If you are the internal champion for a cryptocurrency program, it is a natural expectation that you will also be the one who will be most enthusiastic and knowledgeable about it.

Crypto Lingo

'FUD' → Short for 'fear, uncertainty, doubt', FUD captures the main reasons why many people are hesitant about cryptocurrencies and blockchain technology. While not exclusively a crypto term, it is often used when mainstream investors or companies choose not to get involved.

Preparing for Common Questions

We tend to see the same questions when speaking to decision-makers and other stakeholders when it comes to cryptocurrency donation programs. We have compiled the list of the most frequently asked questions we receive and responses that may be helpful for you to use in your own preparation.

In addition to providing knowledgeable responses to questions that are raised around cryptocurrency and blockchains in your organization, you will also need to be aware of common misconceptions. Just as there was a great deal of fear, uncertainty, and doubt that surrounded the early days of the internet, we have seen similar sensationalism around cryptocurrency and blockchain technologies. People will naturally fear what they don't understand, and the efforts that you take in educating others in cryptocurrency will be a valuable investment in time to ensure that everyone is feeling confident in moving ahead.

People will naturally fear what they don't understand

What other organizations are currently accepting Bitcoin and how successful has it been?

Some of the biggest organizations in the nonprofit sector,including United Way Worldwide and American National Red Cross, have implemented programs. Funders such as Fidelity Charitable also accept Bitcoin. The risk now is *not* having a cryptocurrency program and not being considered by donors to receive their gifts. Many major gifts have been made in cryptocurrency, but what's more important is the long-term growth potential to connect crypto donors with our cause and build the relationship with our organization.

How much time will this take and what will it cost?

It will depend on how quickly we can make decisions. If we use a third-party processor and embed a form on our website, the setup is fairly simple and straightforward and can be completed in as little as a week's time.

The costs of accepting cryptocurrencies are limited to, first, the staff time for implementation, and second, the fees for usage of a platform, which are usually embedded in the cost of each individual transaction. These fees are comparable to fees that are charged for credit card processing and are typically lower.

Often, the most time-consuming part of implementing a cryptocurrency fundraising program is securing organizational support and buy-in from leadership, so we'll need to ensure that we start the education process early.

What are the specific benefits to our charity?

Once we have a cryptocurrency program established, a donor who wishes to make a cryptoasset donation will be able to do so without any delays. It will position our charity as an early adopter and serve as the basis for our major gift teams to seek out donors in our city and take advantage of broader opportunities to engage with cryptocurrency communities. An additional benefit is that it will provide an opportunity to future-proof the organization by building the capacity to learn and adopt new and emerging technologies to address our needs.

How many donations will this bring in?

Accepting cryptoassets isn't a guaranteed ticket to financial success, just as accepting online payments or participating in Giving Tuesday does not automatically mean increased revenue. What this offers is an additional channel, and must form part of a larger strategy, which is critical for the general success of any fundraising program, and should include elements of marketing, communications, and stewardship.

Just as donations made through the website are supported through email and social media appeals, there will also need to be messaging that will be necessary to ensure that those who are involved in cryptocurrency communities are aware that this is available.

After receiving our initial gift of cryptocurrency from a donor, we will need to ensure that there are stewardship plans to continue building the relationship with our organization to ensure subsequent engagement.

What are the drawbacks and risks?

As with any project, there are always risks involved and it is important to focus on how these will be mitigated. The most common concerns raised are outlined below:

1) Few donations will be received

   One distinct possibility is that few donations will be received through this channel. That said, the costs are relatively small. In order for the program to succeed, it needs to be part of a broader fundraising strategy that includes marketing. Like any new fundraising channel, it will take time to grow; the return on investment may not be initially significant, but the cost with regards to staffing and resources to get started is very low compared to other initiatives.

2) Currency fluctuations

   Currency fluctuations are relevant if cryptocurrency is being held as an investment, and if that is the case, it should be evaluated according to existing investment policies and risk management processes. This risk can be mitigated by selling any cryptocurrency immediately upon receipt to establish fair market value for receipting and to secure the value of the donation. Just like donations of securities, you'll need a policy on (as the song goes) when to hold them and when to fold them.

3) Brand risk

   There may be a perception that association with cryptocurrency may pose a brand risk. The cryptocurrency market has matured significantly and is no longer considered a fringe technology, acknowledged by government regulators, large corporations, and many well-respected organizations. There is an opportunity to position the adoption of cryptocurrency as an indicator of innovation within our organization. Every organization should have a gift acceptance policy and clearance procedures, particularly if you are concerned about ethical or reputational issues raised by donations of any sort (cash, in-kind, stocks, crypto, etc.) from potentially brand-damaging individuals, corporations, foundations, governments, or other organizations.

Is It Legal?

Yes. The specific regulations and rulings vary by country, but generally donations made in Bitcoin and other cryptocurrencies are treated as in-kind donations.

Isn't Bitcoin Only Used for Crime?

No. Though Bitcoin has been used for illicit purposes, as well as a currency in ransomware attacks, the vast majority of all transactions are normal day-to-day transactions made by people and businesses. It is important to evaluate Bitcoin as a tool for a store of value, and to recognize that it, like cash, can be used for many legal purposes. It is also important to ensure that there are proper internal financial controls, as well as a gift acceptance policy that applies to *all* gifts to our organization. In many countries, Bitcoin exchanges are required to register with local governments as Money Services Businesses and are regulated accordingly.

Doesn't Bitcoin Get "Hacked" All the Time?

Simply put: it doesn't. Bitcoin has never been hacked. Only companies that have built on top of blockchains have been hacked. The "hacks" that are reported in the media are often sensationalized, and when you look closer, it becomes clear that underlying most of these reports is a common thread: poor security practices on the part of organizations. When one website gets hacked, it doesn't mean the internet has been hacked; when one organization's email gets hacked, it doesn't mean "email" was hacked. And though email breaches occur with startling frequency, it doesn't warrant abandoning email;[51] it requires that the practices, training, and education around securing email be changed. Similarly, companies that connect to a blockchain may get hacked, but it doesn't mean that an entire blockchain has been hacked or needs to be abandoned. As part of general security practice for any digital operation, organizations need to take appropriate precautions to secure any private credentials.

Is it Anonymous?

Most cryptocurrencies are "pseudonymous" rather than strictly "anonymous": after all, every single transaction is logged on a public ledger. There are, however, cryptocurrencies that emphasize anonymity and privacy to a greater degree, such as Monero.[52] As an organization, we can specifically choose which cryptocurrencies we accept and which we don't.

Processes for making anonymous donations are already well-established in the charitable sector, as donations can be conducted through a lawyer or a foundation to preserve anonymity. It is also easier to return a Bitcoin donation than one made through an unmarked envelope of cash, or made through a bank transfer, because a Bitcoin donation can't be made without a return address (i.e. a public key).

---

[51] To see if your email has been identified in a breach, check https://haveibeenpwned.com.
[52] Monero, "Monero: A Private Digital Currency."

Don't You Have to Buy an Entire Bitcoin?

No. This is a common misconception. At the time of writing, a single Bitcoin is valued at over $40,000, and we can all be grateful that you do *not* need to buy an entire Bitcoin. Many, if not most, transactions take place in small fractions of a Bitcoin. Bitcoins are divisible to 8 decimal points, and the smallest unit is called a *satoshi*, or one hundred millionth (1/100,000,000) of a Bitcoin.

Aren't Cryptocurrencies Bad for the Climate?

The process of maintaining the public record of cryptocurrencies consumes a significant amount of electricity, used to validate and process transactions, but this will not always be the case.

First, early blockchains like Bitcoin use a method of mining cryptocurrency called Proof of Work which does consume a lot of energy to validate transactions; however, there are newer blockchains starting to use a method called Proof of Stake, which promises to use as much as 99% less electricity.[53]

Second, climate change is not solely due to electricity consumption, but the mix of energy that is consumed. The utilization of non-renewable energy contributes to climate change and addressing this necessitates advocating for effective energy policy, including support for renewable resources.

Third, cryptocurrency can play a key role in the energy ecosystem. Surplus electricity can be costly to manage and the co-location of mining operations in power plants can help provide a viable alternative. For instance, when there is an oversupply of power due to surplus renewable energy, such as wind power generated in the evenings when energy demand is lower, cryptocurrency mining can make use of the surplus.[54] Additionally, there

---

[53] Fairley, "Ethereum Plans to Cut Its Absurd Energy Consumption by 99 Percent."

[54] Martin, "'Getting paid to produce Bitcoins'."

are also projects such as Power Ledger which has created a market for producers of solar and wind energy to trade renewable energy on the blockchain.[55]

Traditional financial systems also consume energy in the construction of buildings, powering of infrastructure, air conditioning, and employee commutes. While some current iterations of blockchains are energy intensive, the meaningful advances that are being made in renewable energy—combined with the developments in blockchain technology to use less electricity—are promising, and we remain optimistic that these trends will continue to make the technology more sustainable.

Should I Invest in Bitcoin?

This question is frequently asked when Bitcoin prices reach all-time highs. In the context of an organizational implementation, it is not a question that is appropriate. The individual decision to invest in Bitcoin (or anything else) is a personal one that requires research and an evaluation of opportunity and risk. Generally speaking, no one should invest any more than they can afford to lose.

Crypto Philanthropists

In 2018, Vitalik Buterin donated $2.4 million worth of Ether to the SENS Research Foundation for research into human longevity and $1 million to GiveDirectly to support refugees in Africa.[56]

---

[55] Power Ledger, "Power Ledger."

[56] Milova, "Vitalik Buterin: The Best Thing to Donate Money to is the Fight Against Aging."

Setting Up Your Donation Program

> *"I knew nothing about cryptocurrency myself, but it just seemed like this was the new frontier. . . and I said, 'Hey—let's do this.' "*
>
> - Tony Stewart, CEO and Co-Founder of Us4Warriors

There are many ways to approach setting up a cryptocurrency donation program. When evaluating models, remember that there is no universal model that applies to all organizations. Just as organizations and fundraising departments allocate and distribute internal resources towards annual giving, major gifts, and gift planning, establishing a crypto donation program needs to take into account your strategic needs and your organizational capacity.

The models outlined below provide some approaches to explore, but they are not mutually exclusive, nor are they exhaustive. New models for implementation continue to emerge and we encourage you to select the ones that make the most sense for you.

When considering how to accept cryptocurrency donations, ensure that you have a good sense of your organizational capacity. Your approach will vary depending on leadership support, technological capacity, and organizational agility. The implementation of a crypto program should take into account how you will do it within a broader organizational strategy and when.

The following approaches are listed in order of complexity of implementation, from the simplest method of working with a third party to using donated cryptoassets for investments.

Accepting Cryptocurrency via a Third-Party Platform

Using a third-party platform is often quick, simple, and straightforward. In this method, your organization won't ever actually possess the cryptocurrency, since you'll be working with a third-party platform that will accept cryptocurrency on your behalf and immediately convert it to fiat currency. The fiat currency is then deposited directly into your organization's bank account. This approach is analogous to using a payment platform like PayPal that would process donations for you and automatically deposit them into your bank account. This type of automated approach is currently favoured by the vast majority of nonprofits as it is convenient for the donor and establishes the fair market value for the issuance of receipts for tax purposes. It is also the least complicated from a technical perspective.

Since you don't directly hold ownership of your cryptoassets, this solution requires a very high degree of trust between your organization and the processor. If the processor goes under or has their operations frozen by government regulations, then your donation might very well be lost. To mitigate this, regular sweeps of cryptocurrency and fiat into wallets and accounts you control are advised.

What Is Market Depth?

In cryptocurrency marketplaces, prices are set only by what buyers are willing to pay and what sellers are willing to sell for. These prices establish the price of an asset. Market depth describes the ability of a market to process large transactions without impacting its price. Typically, exchanges with a larger number of buyers and sellers will have a greater depth, and assets will sell closely to the fair market value.

To illustrate this in a simple example, imagine you need two copies of a used book. If there were only two copies available in the entire world and one copy is priced at $20 and the other is priced at $100, it would cost $120 to purchase both copies with an average cost of $60 for each book. However, if an additional seller had 1,000 copies available at $25, you could ignore the copy priced at $100 and purchase the one copy at $20 and another at $25, for a total of $45 and an average cost of $22.50 for each book. Even if you wanted to purchase an additional 500 copies at $25, your average cost would be $24.99 because there is enough market depth to absorb your order without significantly impacting the average price.

If you receive a large cryptocurrency donation and wish to convert it to fiat, make sure you're selling it on an exchange with sufficient market depth that your sale won't affect the price of the cryptoasset. While this is rarely a worry for cryptoassets with mass adoption (Bitcoin, Ether, etc.), with lesser-known or rarer assets, it may be more of a concern.

If you're anticipating larger gifts over $10,000 arriving via cryptocurrency, ensure that you confirm with the processor that they're able to handle large transactions. You may be required to submit additional verifications on behalf of your organization in order to be eligible for the processing of larger transactions. These verifications are part of "Know Your Customer" and "Anti-Money Laundering" or KYC/AML regulations. This is common in the banking and fintech space, and your senior management and/or board members may be requested to furnish documentation.

What is KYC/AML?

When setting up an account with an exchange, you may encounter the acronyms KYC and AML, which refer to 'Know Your Customer' and 'Anti-Money Laundering'.

These regulations vary by country, but generally KYC refers to the obligations of a financial institution to conduct due diligence when setting up accounts so they know who they are transacting with. These processes may involve identity verification and confirmation of organizational leadership. In jurisdictions with stringent KYC regulations, you may also be asked by an exchange to provide identity verification from all members of your board in order to set up an account.

AML guidelines generally govern institutional practices around the prevention of money laundering and other financial crimes, such as reporting suspicious activity or large transactions (typically $10,000 or over). From a nonprofit standpoint, these responsibilities typically rest with exchanges and financial institutions. Depending on where you are located, your organizations may be required to disclose details of large gifts, particularly from foreign funding sources, as part of their regular reporting requirements and tax filings to the government. Check with your own tax, legal, and accounting advisors.

Questions to ask a prospective third-party platform:

1) What cryptocurrencies can I accept with your service?
2) Are you a regulated exchange?
3) What are the methods of withdrawal that are available?
4) Do you charge fees to withdraw?
5) What are your withdrawal minimums and limits?
6) What is your capacity to process large gifts?
7) What customer support do you provide?
8) What are your processing fees?
9) What are your security measures?

Pros

- Simple and straightforward setup

Cons

- Potentially high exchange fees
- Requires a high degree of trust with the processor
- Limited to cryptocurrencies and tokens that the provider accepts
- Might only be able to withdraw your funds after you reach a minimum amount of donations

Remember, your approach can get more hands-on over time, as you get more confident with the technology.

Accept Directly and Sell

Another approach is to accept cryptocurrency donations directly and then sell the assets on an exchange for fiat. In this model, a donor would be provided with the organization's public wallet address to which they could send their cryptocurrency. From there, the organization would manage the sale of the assets. This approach is less commonly employed right now, but will likely be used more frequently in the future, when charities are more comfortable with cryptocurrencies. This method requires staff members who are familiar with cryptocurrencies and the corresponding security procedures needed for safely maintaining and using digital wallets. Checks and balances should also be employed that are typically used for financial transactions, such as having two unrelated staff members processing gifts and verifying transactions. In addition, any published addresses should be monitored by multiple individuals to provide additional checks and balances.

If you are an organization that has staff who are tech-savvy or are expecting large gifts of cryptocurrency, this method offers more control and flexibility than using an automated third party.

Pros

- Secure when coupled with checks and balances
- Free to implement
- Your organization keeps a high amount of the donation
- Greater degree of control over the process

Cons

- Requires tech-savvy staff members who are familiar with crypto
- Risk of currency fluctuation if gifts come in over weekends or holidays

Accept and Hold

The choice to accept and hold cryptocurrency should reflect what is outlined in your organization's investment policy. Whether it is managing securities or cryptocurrencies, each organization will need to assess their appetite for risk against their goals. Some organizations that decide to include cryptocurrencies as part of a diversified portfolio may choose to accept and hold these donations in the anticipation that the value will appreciate. From this perspective, the holding of cryptocurrencies can be a portfolio strategy for your organization. As with any asset class, risk must be assessed against opportunity, and in the case of cryptocurrencies, organizations that see it as an investment opportunity may choose to hold over a longer term. As with all cryptocurrency holders, organizations holding cryptoassets should consult a financial professional regarding their local tax codes and keep detailed records of transactions and dates, as certain jurisdictions may tax cryptoasset appreciation at the time of sale (or grant tax breaks in the case of asset depreciation).

As with any asset class, risk must be assessed against opportunity

---

Another benefit of accepting and holding is that, if relevant, the organization may purchase goods and services or transfer funds to beneficiaries directly using cryptocurrency, and also provide full visibility to the donor on how their donation was spent.

If you are an organization that is anticipating significant donations from early-stage cryptocurrency projects or have a diversified investment portfolio, this approach may be one to consider.

Pros

- Potential for significant long-term gains
- Opportunity to engage with early-stage crypto projects to secure early donations before a potential rise in value
- Donors will be more inclined to give to an organization that isn't going to sell right away for fiat

Cons

- Higher risk

Future Forward Fundraising

> *"It's not always common that we get these opportunities, but to be willing to say, 'Look, we took a risk and that risk did pay off,' I think that's where the magic is."*
>
> - Jim Carter III, Founder of Cause Hack

We've outlined the most common approaches nonprofits will take to launch a program. However, there are emerging and experimental approaches to keep an eye on. Just as the internet existed for many years before payment processors like PayPal were widely available, we anticipate that advanced cryptocurrency and blockchain functionality will become more accessible to nonprofits in the coming years.

Automated Matching

Matching programs can be a powerful driver for encouraging donations. Imagine if you could see your donation being processed in real-time and immediately confirm that a matching amount was also deposited into the account of the charity you are supporting. Cryptocurrency smart contracts provide the technology to set up automated matching programs with full transparency for all parties. For example, a smart contract can be programmed to match all donations, and if a certain total amount is met, an additional donation is unlocked.

Crypto Lingo

'Smart contract' ⟶ An automated software-based contract that runs on the blockchain. For example, a donor could set up a smart contract that would hold cryptocurrency until a particular target is reached by the organization. A third party is typically needed to facilitate this type of transaction, but with a smart contract, it can all be automated. Currently, smart contracts are most prevalent on the Ethereum blockchain.

Quadratic Funding

The brightest minds in the cryptocurrency space are looking beyond replicating traditional philanthropy and are creating brand new models, embracing the full potential of cryptocurrency to reimagine donations at their very core.

Quadratic funding is an advanced form of matching donations that supports projects with a greater number of contributors over projects that may have raised more dollars. For example, in a normal matching scenario, if Project A raises $100 from 100 donors ($1 each), it would receive $100 in matching. Similarly, Project B, which also raised $100, but from a single donor, would receive $100 in matching funds. Using quadratic funding, Project A would receive a higher proportion of the matching funding because it had support from a higher number of community members, even if they gave less from a monetary standpoint. The model helps ensure that one wealthy donor doesn't overpower the voice of a community that has less money available to contribute. Quadratic funding models can be built into smart contracts to automate this process in order to prioritize community participation and incentivize collective coordination.[57] An example of an early adopter of the quadratic funding model is Gitcoin Grants,[58] where open source projects are funded. Since its launch in November 2017, Gitcoin Grants has facilitated over $10 million in funding for over 1,275 projects, all with a median donation of $2.75.[59]

---

57 Buterin et al., "Liberal Radicalism: A Flexible Design For Philanthropic Matching Funds."

58 Gitcoin, "Gitcoin Grants."

59 Gitcoin, "$10,231,373 of Funding for Open Source Software."

Crypto Lingo

'Oracles' ⟶ Third-party providers that supply validated information for smart contracts. For instance, rainfall insurance for an outdoor charity event typically needs to be administered by an insurance company. In the future, something like rainfall insurance could be administered by a smart contract connected to an oracle, like a weather report. If the report stated that rain fell in a particular geographic area, it would trigger an automatic payment.

Cryptoasset Trusts

A smart contract can be used to establish a fully transparent cryptoasset trust, which can be configured to release a portion of funds according to pre-set parameters. A simple contract can establish that a certain percentage of an endowment may be released to an organization each year. Individuals may also contribute to a pool of resources that is coded to be automatically distributed to a group of eligible organizations. Caution is required with any type of endowment in perpetuity, because they are set up for the very long term, while charity needs may change over years or decades.

Decentralized Autonomous Organizations

A decentralized autonomous organization (DAO) refers to a complex smart contract that people can send funds into and receive voting power in exchange. For example, a DAO can be developed on the Ethereum network that would allow a group of individuals to pool their money together for a purpose, perhaps to offer microloans. A complex smart contract would take votes from participants on which projects should receive the money, then automatically and transparently distribute the funds. While these functions may be available on other platforms, DAOs are unique in that they are designed to eliminate the need for intermediaries.

Mining and Staking

Mining and staking are the mechanisms that ensure that cryptocurrencies and blockchains continue to update and operate around the world. Mining is a process in which cryptocurrencies are created and transactions are verified by computers and added to the blockchain. Staking is the next generation of the mechanism to verify transactions, and has the advantages of being faster and using less electricity. Participants in mining and staking processes receive fees and/or rewards of cryptocurrency to incentivize their participation.

While it may not be viable for most nonprofits to directly take part in large-scale mining or staking, due to the technical requirements and capital investment needed for it to be profitable, there have been some explorations around donating spare computer processing power for charities.[60] Another opportunity that may be possible in the future is the potential for partnerships with those who are involved directly in cryptocurrency mining or staking, similar to how corporate partners are sought out and cultivated. Just as organizations may seek to align their core business with a social cause, a crypto-savvy nonprofit may be well-equipped to broach a conversation with a cryptocurrency mining or staking operation.

Crypto Philanthropists

The Children's Heart Unit Fund, a UK-based charity that supports children with cardiac ailments, announced in July 2020 that it received nearly $48,000 in donations made using cryptocurrencies.[61]

[60] Cudo Donate, "Donate your idle computer time to Charity."
[61] Kalra, "Children's Heart Charity Receives $48K in Crypto Donations."

Initial Steps

> *"We're still learning and growing, but we do try to keep this cryptocurrency avenue in our mind when we think about fundraising strategies."*
>
> - Henah Parikh, Development and Communications Manager at She's the First

As you launch a cryptocurrency donation program, take into consideration how you will integrate it across your organization. The most successful cryptocurrency programs take into account the needs of various departments and existing functions. Coordinating across departments ensures that your program is not operating in a silo and that you are building a program that provides not only the best possible experience for the donor, but also for your colleagues.

Cryptocurrency Donation Workflow

After a cryptocurrency donation is made, it is helpful to know the specific steps that typically need to occur. A sample workflow is provided below:

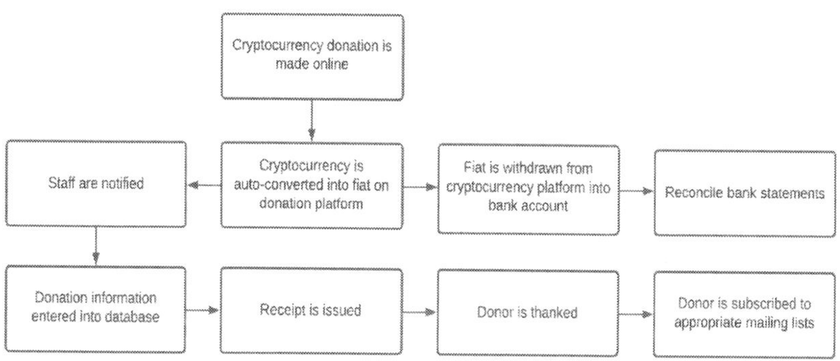

Notification Systems

When a donation is made, ensure that appropriate staff are notified so that subsequent actions may be taken. If you are using a platform to accept and sell donations, this will likely come in the form of an email notification every time a donation is made. If you are accepting cryptocurrency directly, there should be a process to check the accounts regularly to determine if any donations have been made.

If your cryptocurrency donation platform does not automatically issue a tax receipt, ensure that your team has a process for being notified of donations and issuing a receipt.

Website

Your website will often be the primary resource for many donors who are learning more about your cause, and if you offer options to donate cryptocurrency online, this should be easy to find. Cryptocurrency options are often outlined in "Other Ways to Give" on nonprofit websites. Ensure that you coordinate with the staff member responsible for updating the website to post the relevant embed codes for donation forms and/or donation addresses.

The process of making a cryptocurrency gift on your website should be as simple and straightforward as possible. A donor should be able to clearly identify how to donate and complete the transaction seamlessly by scanning a QR code or entering your wallet address.

Fundraising Database

Just as donations are imported and tracked into a donor database, ensure that there is a regularly scheduled process for importing and synchronizing donations that are made via your cryptocurrency channels. Donations made in cryptocurrency should also be clearly identified for tracking and later data analysis.

Finance

Ensure that your finance department is aware of the platform you are using to accept cryptocurrency donations and that they know what to look out for when donations arrive when they are deposited so that it is tracked. If your organization is using a hard wallet, the finance department is typically best suited to store the wallet and recovery seed, as they likely already have procedures for the storage of cash and sensitive documents.

> **Crypto Philanthropists**
>
> Wally Tsuha, a business executive, donated 2 bitcoin (~$50,000) to The Salvation Army - Hawaiian & Pacific Islands as a part of their 2020 Crypto Kettle drive.[62]

[62] Carpenter, "Salvation Army Hawaii lands generous 'crypto kettle' donation."

Policies

> *"Charities are conservative about finances . . . We're so focused on what we know and what's easy that investing in something that's potentially risky or higher cost, that all gets put to put aside for 'let's stick with what we know.'"*
>
> - Ken Wyman, Consultant and Professor Emeritus of the Fundraising Management graduate program at Humber College

Clear policies are powerful tools that organizations can use to govern cryptocurrency programs and provide direction for staff members. They can help prepare for the future by ensuring a consistent approach and reinforcing the structures needed for continuity. However, the addition of a cryptocurrency donation program to your organization does not mean that an entirely separate set of policies needs to be written. In many cases, additions to existing gift acceptance, investment, and internal control policies may be sufficient.

The addition of a cryptocurrency donation program to your organization does not mean that an entirely separate set of policies needs to be written

---

Gift Acceptance Policies

A gift acceptance policy is a helpful resource for an organization to provide clear guidance to staff on gifts that are consistent with its mission. In addition to identifying the types of gifts that are accepted, it will also clearly outline the parameters for when gifts will not be accepted. Considerations that are often taken into account include values of the organization, the type of gift, and the effect that the gift will have on the brand and on future gifts. It should also outline the process for dealing with potentially controversial gifts. When considering the addition of cryptocurrency to a gift acceptance policy, organizations should take into account the treatment of anonymous cryptocurrency gifts. If the question arises around what you would do with an anonymous donation of cryptocurrency, it is worth thinking about how your organization would treat an unmarked envelope of cash. The ethical and procedural considerations around the processing of such a gift may help inform your process around how you would treat a digital version of anonymous cash.

Crypto History

In 2020, members of the hacking group Darkside attempted to donate some of their ransomware proceeds to charity. A donation of 0.88 bitcoin valued at $10,400 was made to Children International. However, a Children International representative indicated that the organization refused the donation.[63]

Investment Policies

An investment policy should provide details around how institutional funds are managed and invested. The policy should provide broad guidelines that inform investment decisions, including goals for returns, and should detail the types of investments that are acceptable and prohibited. To offer clarity, it should specifically include cryptocurrency in addition to other assets, such as securities and real estate, that may be donated.

When it comes to selling cryptocurrency, your approach will be informed by your existing gift acceptance and investment policies. Many organizations opt to sell immediately upon receipt to secure the value of the

[63] Tidy, "Mysterious 'Robin Hood' hackers donating stolen money."

gift and put it to use. This is common, especially if it has been established in practice by the treatment of securities donations. However, there are occasions that may warrant holding over the longer term and specific parameters will need to be outlined in an investment policy.

Internal Controls

Existing internal control policies for an organization will typically outline how an organization will manage the risk around assets. Procedures around internal controls will outline how to prevent and detect fraud. Existing policies may outline procedures regarding the segregation of duties among staff members when it comes to handling cash. Similar principles may be applied to the handling of cryptocurrency. No single staff member should have control over the entire process. For instance, if you are accepting cryptocurrency via a third-party platform and converting it to fiat, ensure that notifications are sent to multiple parties.

Wallet Management Policies

When considering cryptocurrency wallet management policies, if you are using a cold wallet, consider existing cash handling procedures, which may help identify individuals who may be custodians within your organization. As well, when it comes to standard cash handling procedures, two people are typically required during the transport of cash, and detailed records are kept for deposits and withdrawals.

Within an organization, if a cold wallet is used, it should be established who will hold the physical wallet, who will have access to PIN numbers, and where the seed will be stored.

To maintain internal controls:

- The person storing the physical wallet should not be the same person using it to make transactions

- No transaction should be able to be completed without the presence of, or input from, at least two individuals

One way this may be accomplished is that one person holds the cold wallet, while the other holds the PIN to access the wallet. In addition, the public addresses should be known to multiple staff so that transactions can be monitored via a public channel for transparency and visibility. Automated alerts should also be set up to send notifications for activity on any wallets that are connected to a hardware device held by the organization. Careful succession planning, including legally-binding agreements, is essential, in case one or more of these individuals leaves your organization, is engaged in a dispute, or is not available at an important moment for a transaction. Copies of seeds should be kept in a sealed envelope and in a bank safe deposit box (if available) or in another secure off-site location. Seeds should never be sent or stored online, as they will grant whoever accesses them full access to your wallet and its contents.

Crypto Philanthropists

In 2011, the Bitcoin100 project was created on Bitcointalk.org with a goal of bringing greater awareness to Bitcoin. Over five years, until its conclusion in 2016, it provided donations of 681 bitcoins across 83 charities.[64]

[64] Gage, "Re: Bitcoin 100 has run its course."

Security

> *"I prefer a more anonymous style of giving. I don't like the publicity portion of it—that's not why I do it."*
>
> - Andrew, Crypto Donor and Investor

Securing cryptocurrency requires vigilance and planning from your entire organization. A shared sense of the importance of cybersecurity is important, but vigilance about basic security practices is just as vital. After all, what is the point of having a safe to store your valuables if you don't lock the front door?

Managing security is about managing the risks to your organization, and when it comes to the digital age and cryptocurrencies, cybersecurity is key. Cybersecurity risk mitigation needs to be embedded within every aspect of an organization, from onboarding to day-to-day operations. While this book is not intended to be a comprehensive resource, it is worthwhile to ensure that your organization is embracing the latest best practices when it comes to securing your information. The considerations below are framed in the context of a cryptocurrency donation program, but apply to general security considerations as well.

Cybersecurity risk mitigation needs to be embedded within every aspect of an organization, from onboarding to day-to-day operations

---

Storing Crypto

A productive way of thinking about security is to assume you are already hacked. When this assumption is made, additional precautions can be taken to mitigate risks. Some malware, once installed, will silently monitor computers for the existence of private keys and the instant that it is found, the cryptocurrency may be lost. For this reason, cold wallets and hardware wallets are generally accepted to be the most secure way to store cryptocurrency. It is not recommended to store cryptocurrency on any exchange beyond the time needed to process your transactions. Doing so is antithetical to the generally held principles of cryptocurrency and decentralization. As the saying goes, "not your keys, not your coins." You wouldn't leave a pile of cash in an unlocked desk drawer, so be equally cautious with your crypto.

Password Management

If you use the same password across multiple websites, you need to take immediate action. The number of passwords divulged from security breaches is in the billions. You can verify if you have been breached via websites like *Have I Been Pwned.* A weak password is an easy target to a determined hacker. Passwords should be unique to each platform or exchange, and a password manager should be employed to ensure that you are using unique passwords with random characters.

A password manager allows you to store all of your account passwords in an encrypted account and protect it with two-factor authentication (as mentioned in the earlier section on Exchanging Your Money). This software provides a browser extension that you can use on the internet to generate passwords with random characters and securely store them. The software will then auto-fill your credentials on websites and you can rest assured that if one website is breached, because you're not duplicating passwords, you don't have to worry about having all of your accounts compromised.

Two-Factor Authentication

Two-factor authentication is critical for ensuring that even if the password is somehow discovered or breached, that access will still not be granted. Two-factor authentication refers to the need for two different types of things to verify identity in order to gain access, which may include:

- Something you know (e.g. a password)
- Something you have (e.g. a phone or security key)
- Something you are (e.g. a fingerprint)
- Somewhere you are (e.g. an IP address or GPS location)

Two-factor authentication ensures that even if a password is known, an attacker would also need to have access to another factor of authentication, which makes it more difficult to compromise a system. While SMS-based two-factor authentication may be available and may serve as a basic protection, this is vulnerable to attacks and social engineering. It is recommended that you use an authenticator app or a hardware authentication device.

Authenticator Apps and Hardware Authentication Devices

An authenticator app is a mobile app that is used to verify identity. When setting up an online account, this may be an option for two-factor authentication that provides additional security by providing an additional numerical passcode that changes frequently. Once it is set up, the combination of your password and the numerical code on your authenticator app will grant you access to your account. Authenticator apps are digital versions of physical security tokens that rotate a six-digit code every minute, and which are often used for safeguarding access to databases containing personal information.

A hardware authentication device is a physical, electronic "key" that you keep on you to verify your identity. These devices may be plugged into your computer via a USB port or may utilize NFC technology so that they can be tapped against an NFC reader on your mobile device. This is generally considered to be one of the most secure ways to protect online accounts.

Wallet Storage

Generally, the finance department of an organization will retain control over a physical wallet and procedures will need to be established to ensure that there are multiple checks and balances. The physical storage of any hardware wallet will need to be treated with the same care and consideration as with storing cash equivalents. Generally speaking, a thought experiment that will aid in determining the effectiveness of your financial controls is to ask how you and your staff would handle the keys to a safe deposit box.

Social Engineering

While hacking is often perceived to be technical in nature, a hacker may use social engineering to take advantage of vulnerabilities in organizational processes and individual behaviours to achieve their goals. It is important that staff are aware of social engineering tactics that may be employed to gain access to credentials. For instance, rather than trying to hack an account directly, a hacker may attempt to call a cell phone provider and impersonate someone with details gleaned from the internet in order to bypass security protocols.

Fraudulent attempts to obtain sensitive information are referred to as phishing and may take the form of falsified emails pretending to be from colleagues, vendors, or exchanges and/or prompting a user to visit a fraudulent website and enter their credentials. Phishing emails that prompt users to click on documents may be employed to gain access to networks. More advanced tactics may involve personalized emails or even phone calls that may request urgent action in order to override established protocols.

Crypto Philanthropists

Sam Bankman-Fried, the CEO of cryptocurrency derivatives platform FTX, made the second-largest donation to Joe Biden's presidential campaign, totalling $5.2 million.[65]

[65] Sinclair, "Cryptocurrency CEO Donated Second-Largest Amount to Joe Biden's Campaign."

Tax and Accounting Considerations

> *"If you're a public charity why not make all your accounting— at least the Bitcoin side of it— completely public so that people don't have to trust you. They can just look at the blockchain."*
>
> - Michael Tozoni, Treasurer of Bitcoin100

In 2019, the US Internal Revenue Service's 1040 tax form asked those filing the following question: "At any time during 2019, did you receive, sell, send, exchange, or otherwise acquire any financial interest in any virtual currency?" This was an indication that tax authorities were finally taking cryptocurrency seriously. Since cryptocurrency was introduced, governments have contended with its regulation, including taxation and reporting requirements for both individuals and organizations. Cryptocurrencies have also emerged in questionnaires that tax regulators use to audit charities. Below are some sample questions from a charity audit that this book will help you prepare to answer:[66]

1) During the audit period, did you own cryptocurrencies?
2) What was the estimated total cost of the cryptocurrencies you acquired?
3) How do you keep purchase and sale records for cryptocurrency?
4) Do you accept cryptocurrencies as a form of donation?
5) Describe the flow of funds for a typical transaction.
6) How do you account for the sale in your accounting system?
7) How do you determine the fiat equivalent for your books and records?
8) Which bank accounts are linked with your receipts and payments of cryptocurrencies?

---

[66] Blumberg, "CRA asking about cryptocurrencies on charity audits."

In addition to the questions above that pertain to your organization's processes, you will also need to be aware of some of the basic tax regulations that are applicable to donors, such as capital gains.

Capital Gains Regulations for Donors and for Charities

One of the most frequently asked questions regarding donations to charities is whether donations are subject to capital gains. If a donor purchased cryptocurrency and its value appreciates 100x over a few years, they would be responsible for capital gains taxes upon selling it. However, if the cryptocurrency were donated directly to a charity, it could provide benefits to the donor: first, by allowing the full value of the donation to be realized, and second, by allowing the donor to potentially claim a tax deduction based on the fair market value of the donation, depending on their country's tax laws.

Since cryptocurrency was introduced, governments have contended with its regulation, including taxation and reporting requirements

---

The treatment of capital gains varies by country in this regard. As of January 2021, while the US, UK, and Australia offer capital gains exemptions for donations of cryptocurrency to registered charities, Canada does not. For Canadians, this has meant that individuals who donate cryptocurrency are responsible for capital gains taxes associated with the transaction. As regulations are still evolving around capital gains treatment, it is recommended that individuals consult with local financial professionals to assess their obligations.

Receipting

While specific local regulations differ across countries, issuing tax receipts for donations of cryptocurrency is straightforward once fair market value has been established. If you are using a platform that automatically converts cryptocurrencies to fiat, you can simply take the converted value in your local currency and use that amount on the tax receipt. Some platforms that are designed specifically for charities may even issue the tax receipt on your behalf. However, if you are receiving a donation of cryptocurrency directly, you will need to document the date that you received the donation and the fair market value of the gift at the time it was made. Any increase or decrease in value after that point is irrelevant for tax receipting purposes. The receipt is for the full value with no deduction for processing fees.

Fair Market Value

Fair Market Value is needed to issue any tax receipt. If you are issuing a receipt for someone who donates a bitcoin (or anything else), the government wants to know that the value that you have printed on the tax receipt is legitimate and that you haven't arbitrarily made up a number. For example, if someone donates 1 bitcoin and you issue a tax receipt for $1,000,000, you would need to be able to support that valuation with evidence that it was a fair assessment. Assuming that there are no reasonable buyers willing to pay $1,000,000 (yet!) for a single bitcoin, you will have to figure out the best price you can get for it online, and that number should match up to the number you provide on the tax receipt. Establishing fair market value is straightforward on cryptocurrency exchanges, as they are designed specifically to match buyers and sellers.

Crypto Philanthropists

In 2019, the Zcash Foundation donated 1,044.41369 ZEC (equivalent to $40,000 at the time of donation) to Open Privacy, a Canadian nonprofit that works on permissionless privacy tools.[67]

Set Up Your Program Checklist

❏ Organize a general education session for key decision-makers about cryptocurrencies and their potential

❏ Secure support from your executive and/or board to launch a program

❏ Organize a general education session about cryptocurrencies for your team

❏ Educate relevant team members on the plan for the program and how they fit into the process

❏ Determine the structure of the program you want to have, including:

❏ How you accept the donation of cryptocurrencies

❏ How and when you sell cryptocurrencies

❏ How you store cryptocurrencies

❏ Define the process that donors and their donations will follow, including:

❏ Unique coding in the donor database

❏ Treatment within the finance department's accounting processes

❏ Ownership over the relationship of the donors

❏ Prepare any necessary policies around security, private keys, and wallet management

❏ Evaluate different third-party processors or wallet options based on your needs and select the one that is best

[67] Mann, "Zcash Foundation Donation to Open Privacy."

- ❑ Open a wallet and safely backup the private keys according to your wallet management policy (as required)
- ❑ Evaluate different exchange options based on your needs and select the one that is best (as required)
- ❑ Open an account with the selected exchange and at least one other as a backup (as required)
- ❑ Build out your donation website, including your donation QR codes and an FAQ section
- ❑ Run test transactions, including (as relevant):
- ❑ Donating via your website QR codes
- ❑ Sending crypto from your wallet to your exchange and back
- ❑ Converting crypto to fiat in your exchange account
- ❑ Withdrawing fiat from your exchange to your bank account
- ❑ Communicate with the whole organization about the upcoming launch, being sure to address key concerns about cryptocurrencies
- ❑ Soft launch your donation page and retest functionality

III: Get the Gift

The Crypto Community and Philosophy

> *"It's not about the technology, it's the philosophy behind it. Bitcoin is a new form of doing things."*
>
> - Alejandro, Crypto Donor

The cryptocurrency community is one of the most distinctive donor communities in the world. Born out of the cypherpunk movement and united by a common philosophy, the collective of crypto enthusiasts, entrepreneurs, and die-hards that make up the global blockchain community is one of extraordinary individuals—both in their talents and accomplishments, and in their viewpoints.

Early adopters of Bitcoin often carry deep Libertarian roots. While globally a diverse set of philosophies, in this sense we mean the dominant style of American Libertarianism, which values freedom of choice, free markets, and individual judgement. Followers of the philosophy are generally opposed to government regulation and intervention in markets and are activists for the reduction in the size—and more importantly, power—of government. Libertarians believe, for example, that taxation as a means of wealth distribution is coercive and unjustified. They are also in favour of personal autonomy and strong private property rights, including the right to own and carry guns. For these reasons, Libertarians are often labelled as extremely right-wing in their political leanings; however, this label is, in many cases, flawed. Because of their belief in self-sovereignty and individual rights, Libertarians strongly support civil liberties and many of the causes backed by left-leaning political ideologies, including the decriminalization of drugs, marriage rights for the LGBTQ2IA+ community, and open borders, while opposing actions like military interventions and racial discrimination.

While it may not seem like it at first, this mindset is prime for charitable giving. Libertarians are people who are staunchly passionate about their causes, and believe they should have the right to choose which cause their money goes to.

Crypto Lingo

'Taxation is theft' ⟶ A Libertarian slogan often heard in Bitcoin circles that describes the belief that governments should not be able to tax citizens.

Since the growth of the industry, and the inclusion of new blockchains besides Bitcoin, the mindset of the community has broadened. Many individuals see blockchains not only as the back-end technology of Bitcoin, but also as a means to redesign governance structures and other centralized social systems. Reimagining the structure of our societies' services into ones that are decentralized is a means to put power back into the hands of ordinary citizens.

What's key to understand about the members of this unique community is that they are all working to conceive, build, and grow a technology as a part of a decentralized global network of people. Their desire to see the success of this technology is not about personal gain, although that will come with it; it's about believing in and contributing to something greater than themselves—much like many people working in the charitable sector.

Their desire to see the success of this technology is not about personal gain . . .it's about believing in and contributing to something greater than themselves

Many of these projects are transparent, open-source initiatives. As such, the value of community is significant to the success of both building the technology, and also ensuring its adoption at a global level. Blockchain and crypto projects take a great deal of time, and those who run them put significant effort into building, stewarding, and supporting their communities. Crypto donors will be watching how you treat your donor community, and your standard will not be measured against other charities; it will be measured against what they are used to in the blockchain world, which is a high bar.

In order to get a full understanding of what it's like to participate in a crypto community, consider choosing a particular blockchain project, company, or initiative, and joining their community groups. Often these groups will be on Slack, Telegram, Twitter, and Discord, although the platforms are constantly changing with the needs and desires of the community.

Crypto Philanthropists

Bail Bloc gives all of the funds generated by its users mining the cryptocurrency Monero to the Bronx Freedom Fund, which pays bail for people who can't afford it and might lose their job or custody of their children as a result of jail time.[68]

[68] Robitzski, "Charity Lets You Mine Monero to Post Bail."

Crypto Donor Profiles

> *"One thing I noticed about the crypto community is that there are a lot of outlaws in there. I mean that in a favourable way—everyone's a bit rogue."*
>
> - Tony Stewart, CEO and Co-Founder of Us4Warriors

Many charities will have a profile for their "average donor"—the gender, age, and other properties of the people who are more likely to make gifts to their organization. In targeting crypto donors, a smart fundraiser will throw that profile out the window. Getting a crypto gift will require you to look at the community with a completely open mind about who may be interested in your work and who may have the capacity to make major gifts. Unlike at a typical major donor event, at a crypto event, the person with the most capacity to give might be a 21-year-old wearing a purple unicorn t-shirt.

The crypto community is fairly homogeneous in its demographics. While the proportion of women in the space is higher than ever, it remains the case that more than 90% of people in the space are men.[69] The average Bitcoiner skews quite young, with nearly 50% in the millennial category. In fact, fewer than 5% are above the age of 55. A survey done in 2018 found that usage is highest in European countries,[70] although growth amongst younger users was highest in Africa, Oceania, and the Americas—a potential indicator of future user growth.[71]

Their top five interests on Google include:

- Financial Services/Investment Services

[69] Comben, "Google Analytics Reveal Surprising Bitcoin Demographics."
[70] CoinTraffic, "Crypto Audience Revealed: Who Is Your Target User?"
[71] Helms, "9 Countries Show Huge Growth in Cryptocurrency Interest."

- Software/Design Software/Drawing & Animation Software
- Financial Services/Banking Services
- Employment
- Consumer Electronics/Mobile Phones

They were also most likely to be included in the following groups:

- Avid Investors
- Technophiles
- Shutterbugs
- Movie Lovers
- TV Lovers

Therefore, generally, your average donor in the crypto space is a European male between the ages of 24-35 who likes technology and movies.[72]

Getting a crypto gift will require you to look at the community with a completely open mind about who may . . . have the capacity to make major gifts

---

While the cryptocurrency community is a niche within your existing donor segments, it also has many subsegments that will help you better understand the philosophy of your donor, and subsequently, what issues are important to them and how they like to give. While most donors will fall into multiple categories, they may have a greater affinity for one subcommunity over another.

[72] CoinTraffic, "Crypto Audience Revealed: Who Is Your Target User?"

The Bitcoin Maximalist

Bitcoin Maximalists see Bitcoin as the only crypto token that matters. In their minds, all other tokens are irrelevant. The focus of this subset of the community is solely on Bitcoin and increasing its global adoption. From that perspective, they have a more "activist" mentality—doing everything they can to achieve their agenda. They are less focused on applications of the Bitcoin blockchain other than money. Maximalists typically hold deep Libertarian values. They can be more set in their opinions, and hold viewpoints that are unlikely to change.

Donors who fall into the maximalist category may be more likely to donate to causes that fight for freedom from oppressive governments and support organizations that are independent of government interventions.

Crypto Lingo

'Cypherpunk' ⟶ An individual who strongly believes in the right to personal privacy and advocates for the widespread use of cryptography and encryption algorithms to protect it. They build and distribute privacy-enhancing technologies as a means to create social and political change.

The Decentralist

Decentralists tend to align more with the Ethereum community. While they are still likely to be Libertarian-leaning Bitcoin holders, they are distinct in that they are not necessarily focused on eliminating governments and other social structures, but redesigning them in a decentralized format which removes power from existing institutions and puts it into the hands of the people.

The Ethereum community more overtly values human diversity, actively promoting the inclusion of women and BIPOC in their teams and at their events.

The community often creates whimsical marketing materials for conferences, sometimes even decorating event halls with unicorns and rainbows.

Decentralists are often engaged in building applications that will have a wider impact on society than just money movement. Donors who fall into this category may be attracted to organizations who are supporting underserved communities or are using technology to create social change.

Crypto Lingo

'Pegabufficorn' → The ETHDenver hackathon, hosted annually in Denver, Colorado, used the buffalo as their mascot the first year. In their second year, they upped the ante and thought that a buffalo with a unicorn horn would be better, and introduced a 'bufficorn' mascot. In their third year, a pegasus was mixed in, creating a mascot, the 'Pegabufficorn', that was a flying buffalo with a unicorn horn.

The Developer

Developers are on the technical side of the crypto world—the coders. They are the people building, maintaining, and improving the technology used by the community. They are often interested in solving complex technical problems and looking at new ways of building software to achieve their goals. Donors that fall into this category may be more interested in the practicalities of your programs and how they operate to achieve your overall goal.

The Entrepreneur

Crypto entrepreneurs are on the business side of the industry. Sometimes developers themselves, they lead teams to build and grow applications with a focus not only on the technical benefits, but also on how to raise funds, acquire new users, and build products that will generate revenue. Donors that fall into this category may be more interested in how your organization will scale its work to achieve more significant impact, or will look for innovative approaches to solving social problems.

The Trader

Falling on the financial side of the crypto community, traders are people who buy and sell cryptocurrency to make money—similar to someone who would buy and sell stocks. Often they invest in particular tokens not because they believe in the project or its founders, but because they think market demand will drive prices up so they can buy low and sell high. Donors that fall into this category may be interested in the return on investment of your project.

The Investor

The Investor is someone who not only invests in cryptocurrency, but also makes investments in the companies building applications in the sector. Their goal is to support companies to enable them to grow and achieve impact. They will have more of a business mindset, looking at how one approach to solving a problem may be more effective than another offered by an organization doing similar work to your own.

The Timeline of a Community

One parameter that may help you get an understanding of your donor and which categories they might belong to is to find out what year they got into crypto. While this will only provide generalizations, it can act as a signpost to begin your analysis.

2009-2013 ⟶ Libertarians, cypherpunks, and Bitcoin Maximalists

2014-2016 ⟶ Ethereum supporters and Decentralists

2017 ⟶ Opportunistic investors and traders

2018 onwards ⟶ Early adopters from the general population

Tread lightly with this question, however, as it can be a sensitive topic. Asking what year people got into crypto can be a sign that you are questioning their credibility (based on the faulty assumption that people who have been around longer have more credibility) or trying to find out how much money they might have, as very early adopters are much more likely to have seen a major appreciation in the value of their initial investments.

Once you have researched your potential donor and better understand their values and what potential subgroups they may be a part of, you can design a plan to steward the donor and secure a gift.

Crypto Philanthropists

In 2018, Ripple donated $29 million in XRP tokens to support the purchase of goods for 28,000 public school classrooms across 50 states.[73]

[73] Rooney, "Ripple gives away $29 million of its cryptocurrency to public schools."

Getting the Gift

> *"Charities that are more passive, that accept crypto, but don't tell people about it, don't see as many donations."*
>
> - Alex Wilson, CEO and Co-Founder of The Giving Block

Now that you've got your donation program set up and have a good understanding of the crypto community, it's time to secure your first gift. You'll find that attracting and prospecting for crypto donors will use many of the same strategies as with traditional donors, but with some critical modifications. Below are a few techniques to think about after you've opened your donation site.

Make it Easy for Donors to Find You

In the early days of crypto, few stores or charities accepted Bitcoin as payment. In order to connect people who wanted to spend their Bitcoin with merchants who accepted it as payment, a number of websites popped up, listing where crypto could be spent. Similarly, distinct sites listing charities that accepted Bitcoin were created as well. While Bitcoin is more globally accepted than it used to be, these lists still serve as a resource for crypto owners looking to spend or donate. Getting your organization added to these lists is an easy way to make yourself known to the community as an option for giving.

Search Engine Optimization (SEO) / Search Engine Marketing (SEM)

For donors who are actively looking to donate, a Google search is often the first place they go to see what their options are in terms of charities accepting crypto. A page that explains your cryptocurrency donation program and processes will be helpful for search engine optimization in the event that donors are searching specifically for charities that accept cryptocurrency. If you have access to a program like Google Ad Grants,[74] which provides $10,000 a month in advertising credits, in addition to your branded keywords, consider setting up a campaign that includes keyword phrases such as "charities that accept bitcoin", combined with other keywords that reflect your mission.

Promote Your Program

One of the simplest ways to get crypto donors is to promote your program. Once you are set up to accept donations, prominently display the Bitcoin logo (or Ethereum logo, etc.) on your website with an easy link to make a donation. This will indicate to anyone visiting your site that a crypto donation option is available.

The crypto community is very active on social media sites, particularly Twitter (the community is known as "Crypto Twitter"). Share news about the launch of your program on Twitter using common crypto hashtags including:

- Generally: #crypto, #blockchain, #cryptocurrency
- For Bitcoin donations: #bitcoin, #BTC, $BTC
- For Ether donations: #ethereum, #ether, #ETH, $ETH

Reddit is another social media site where you will find crypto communities. Make postings in subreddits related to the tokens you are accepting:

- Bitcoin:
    - r/bitcoin
    - r/bitcoin_uncensored
    - r/cryptocurrency
- Ethereum:
    - r/ethereum
    - r/ethtrader

[74] Google, "Google AdGrants."

Note that, confusingly, the r/btc subreddit is actually dedicated to Bitcoin Cash, which has the handle @BCH. There are also local Bitcoin subreddits, for example, r/bitcoinUK for the United Kingdom and r/bitcoinCA for Canada.

The crypto community also actively connects online and in person at events called "meetups". These gatherings tend to be low-key social events that occur at a local pub or community space. It's an opportunity for people who are passionate about the technology to meet each other, discuss, and build projects together. Sometimes meetups will feature a speaker who will present on a particular project or topic. Search on meetup.com for local meetups in your area and connect with the organizers to see if you can have some time during one of the meetups to talk about your organization's work and your new crypto donation program.

Crypto Lingo

'Hackathon' ⟶ A hackathon is a tech event where teams of coders come together and compete against one another to take a concept from idea to working prototype, often over the course of a weekend. Winners frequently receive cash prizes and can get noticed by investors or potential employers.

Communications and Public Relations

In certain regions, this type of news might be of particular interest to local media outlets, especially if you are the first organization in your area to do so. Your communications/PR staff should also look into reaching out to crypto media outlets for promotion. You may also wish to coordinate with your fundraising team to identify opportunities to highlight a key donor or partner with a local cryptocurrency exchange for an inaugural donation.

Look Within Your Existing Donors

As with traditional gifts of cash or securities, one of the best places to look for donors is in your database. Your organization may already be supported by a donor who historically has been giving lower-level cash donations, but would be capable of much more significant levels of giving if the organization accepted cryptocurrency. Be sure to connect with all the members of your organization to find out if they recall any donors bringing up Bitcoin in conversation at an event or during a meeting.

One of the easiest ways to find out who in your donor database is a crypto owner is simply to ask! In your next donor survey or e-newsletter, include a question asking if your donors would be interested in making a crypto donation.

Prospect Research

When searching for donor prospects in the news, you will find that crypto is not well covered by traditional media outlets. The cryptocurrency community and industry have their own dedicated global and regional media sources that will be better suited to searching for high-value donors. Those who conduct prospect research in your organization will need to be aware of crypto media outlets. Global coverage is found in outlets like *CoinDesk*, *Bitcoin Magazine*, and *Cointelegraph*. There are also local publications for different regions of the world.

Traditional media outlets that have crypto coverage include *CNBC Cryptocurrency* and *Forbes Crypto & Blockchain.*

[Meetups are] an opportunity for people who are passionate about the technology to meet each other, discuss, and build projects together

---

Major Gifts and Individual Philanthropy

In the cryptocurrency world, there are many individuals who have amassed significant wealth over the past decade. As such, organizations should take this into consideration in their prospect research and it may be helpful to ensure that there is a basic understanding of the crypto community, its philosophy, and market-based giving patterns.

Following major appreciations of cryptocurrency value, there may be a greater possibility of a major gift. If you are anticipating a large donation of cryptocurrency that will need to be converted to fiat, you will likely need to engage an over-the-counter (OTC) service for large gifts in excess of $100,000.

Crypto Lingo

'Over-the-Counter' ⟶ Also known as OTC, over-the-counter cryptocurrency transactions are typically used for large transactions and are conducted directly between trusted parties versus a standard market exchange. For example, if your organization received a donation of cryptocurrency worth $1 million and you tried to sell it on a standard exchange with limited market depth, you may have to conduct multiple transactions to get an optimal price. OTC services will allow you to sell a large block of cryptocurrency directly to a single party. This service is often offered by larger cryptocurrency exchanges and you can expect higher levels of customer support in this process.

Gift Planning

An area that continues to emerge is that of cryptoasset inheritance and gift planning. This concept is noted in resources around Planned Giving by the Canadian Association of Gift Planners.[75] While gift planning encourages donors to consider their end of life planning, cryptocurrency adds an additional layer of complexity. Many cryptocurrency owners haven't considered the need to create a will that specifically addresses their cryptocurrency. Because of the nature of crypto wallets and exchanges, it can be difficult for family members to a) know where to look for assets, b) access assets they know about, and c) know who to trust in order to get support. After someone passes away, it can be difficult—bordering on impossible—to track down private keys and wallet seeds that provide access to cryptoassets. There is a role for fundraisers to bring awareness to cryptoassets with regards to gift planning conversations and to support donors to create a plan. Your team should understand what a cryptoasset will and estate plan looks like and how to help donors create one for their families. We recommend reading Pamela Morgan's *Cryptoasset Inheritance Planning.*[76]

Direct Marketing

Your direct marketing program can be a great place to promote your crypto donation program. E-newsletters highlight your capabilities to accept cryptocurrency and you can link to your crypto donation page on your website. If your organization engages in a direct mail program, depending

[75] CAGP, "Planned Giving for Canadians (eBook)."
[76] Morgan, "Cryptoasset Inheritance Planning: A Simple Guide for Owners."

on your audience, you may consider including an option to pay via cryptocurrency with QR codes prominently displayed with the corresponding cryptocurrency's logo.

Corporate Philanthropy

Depending on what specific programs your organization offers, you may have the opportunity to partner with or receive sponsorship from cryptocurrency and blockchain companies. When considering corporate engagement, explore opportunities with cryptocurrency software companies, exchanges, and miners. Also, if your research uncovers companies who may be paying their staff in cryptocurrency, this may provide an additional opportunity for your corporate philanthropy team to engage an organization's employees.

Crypto History

In 2018, KFC Canada ran a promotion to accept Bitcoin payments for buckets of chicken. Customers would receive a bucket of 10 chicken tenders, waffle fries, a side dish, gravy, and two dips.[77] Following the promotion, the Bitcoin proceeds were donated to Pathways to Education Canada.

[77] Shaw, "No joke: KFC Canada starts accepting Bitcoin for a bucket of chicken, immediately sells out."

Grants

There are millions of dollars in grants available from various organizations looking to support the ecosystem.[78] While most of them have a specific focus on technical developments to grow the functionality and use of particular blockchains, many have community-oriented support and may be a fit for certain niche organizations. Grant researchers will need to become familiar with some of the major blockchain foundations, their granting style and schedule, and more importantly, how and where these grant announcements are communicated.

Stewardship and Donor Support

Your donor support team will need to create specific thank you letters and stewardship updates for the crypto community that recognize their unique giving. The team will also need to be prepared to handle support inquiries to help people who are newer to crypto to complete their donations and deal with any donation issues that arise.

Back to Basics

Cryptocurrency donors, while unique in their own way, are still donors. Don't forget to use the strategies you already have in place to acquire, cultivate, and convert ordinary donors and apply them to this new group. As crypto adoption grows and the community expands, you'll find that the quirks and niche elements of today's community may be less pronounced. You'll also find that more of your traditional donors will begin to carry cryptocurrencies as a part of their portfolios.

---

[78] Wright, "Ethereum Foundation announces $3.8M in new grants."

Crypto Philanthropists

Nikolai Mushegian, a key contributor to stablecoin MakerDAO, donated 10,000 MKR tokens (approximately $4.3 million) to his alma mater, Carnegie Mellon University, to develop a research program in decentralized finance and game theory.[79]

[79] Post, "Carnegie Mellon University Sees $4M Pledge to Develop DeFi Research Program."

Crypto Impact and Use Cases for the Nonprofit Sector

> *"We're using crypto and following it on the blockchain to benefit from being able to transfer funds globally much cheaper, faster, and more transparently."*
>
> - Connie Gallippi, Founder and Executive Director of BitGive

After you've successfully set up a cryptocurrency program, you are in an ideal position to explore the many other ways that blockchain technology can help serve your beneficiaries and create social change. Accepting cryptocurrencies is just the beginning of a broader conversation. In addition to being able to facilitate a reliable digital store of value, the public, decentralized, and immutable aspects of blockchains provide practical functionality.

The underlying technology that is used for cryptocurrency donations is changing the social impact space. Just as the internet itself has provided a space for apps, marketplaces, websites, and payments, blockchain technology is providing a foundation on which additional transformative technologies may be built. In the next few years, we will see the creativity and unique needs of communities and nonprofits reflected as the technologies continue to mature and unfold. Here are some other areas in which your organization may be able to benefit more broadly from blockchain technology in the future:

Humanitarian Aid Distribution

Beyond donations, one of the most direct applications of cryptocurrency is utilizing its key functions as a store of wealth that can be sent digitally. Historically, international aid workers have had to deal with transporting, storing, and securing large amounts of cash in order to pay local vendors and partners. This is not only inconvenient, but also presents a significant security risk. By using cryptocurrencies, organizations working in international development can mitigate security concerns that might otherwise surface around transferring payments digitally or with cash.

In May 2019, Oxfam launched a solution to provide blockchain-based humanitarian cash transfers in Vanuatu as a pilot to explore the potential benefits of blockchain technology. In addition to faster onboarding and reduced intermediaries, another significant outcome of the project was that it could significantly reduce the cost of bank transfers to Vanuatu from $20 (Australian) to about $0.10 when an Ethereum transaction was used.[80]

International Remittance and Cash Transfers

Every year, millions of people send money back to their home countries to support their loved ones. These international remittances serve as important financial bridges for families that are spread across the world and directly support over 800 million people worldwide.[81] Remittances are one of the biggest sources of poverty reduction in the world and have a significant impact on people's lives. The World Bank estimated the value of personal remittances at over $650 billion in 2019,[82] and in 2020 the global average cost was 6.75% of the amount transferred, with an average cost of 10.89% among banks. Sub-Saharan Africa remains the most expensive region to send money, at 8.47% in Q3 2020.[83] In other terms, out of the average transfer of $200, $16 of that will go to pay for fees. When you consider that remittances are sent every one or two months by migrant workers, this adds up. The usage of cryptocurrencies and blockchain technology provides the ability to transmit money without barriers and marks a significant advancement in financial technology.

---

80 Consensys, "Project Unblocked Cash: Blockchain Case Study for NGOs."

81 IFAD, "Sending Money Home."

82 The World Bank, "Personal remittances, received (current US$)."

83 The World Bank, "Remittance Prices Worldwide."

Banking the Unbanked

In 2017 there were 1.7 billion adults around the world who remain unbanked.[84] This represents a significant proportion of the world's population who are unable to participate in the broader global economy and can further perpetuate poverty. However, participating in traditional banking systems can present barriers for those who are living in low-income communities due to service charges and monthly fees. Physical banking locations can also be inconvenient for the day-to-day needs of those living in rural and remote areas. There is a great deal of potential for cryptocurrency technologies to aid in ensuring the unbanked can still benefit from participation in financial economies.

Bank Transfers

Sending an international wire transfer is administratively cumbersome, requiring the sender to provide accounting numbers, routing numbers, SWIFT codes, and more. In addition, after this information is provided, it may take several business days for the transfer to be processed and confirmed. While this system has served the world since 1974, blockchain-based solutions can achieve the same outcome of reliably transferring value in minutes, rather than days. For charities who are working with overseas offices and/or vendors, utilizing the blockchain for transferring money can provide a significantly streamlined experience.

Public Registries of Ownership

Public registries, such as property records, require using a dedicated database or going to a physical location; however, recording public information on a public blockchain ensures universal availability of the data, and also tracks changes for transparency. Blockchains provide an immutable record and can hold and provide tamper-proof data.

[84] Global Findex, "The Unbanked."

An example of this concept in action is SuperRare, which provides authenticated single-edition digital artworks that are certified on the Ethereum blockchain.[85] As of December 2020, the platform had facilitated more than $4.5 million worth of digital art sales, as well as over $1 million in secondary market sales.

Education

Cryptocurrency has been used to facilitate incentive distributions in education such as the usage of Smileycoin at the University of Iceland, where the cryptocurrency was distributed based on student participation.[86] In this project, students had the opportunity to receive cryptocurrency that could then be redeemed for cups of coffee, or coupons which could be redeemed for movie tickets, flights, or cellular phone airtime. Interestingly, when students were also offered an option to donate their accrued Smileycoins to support Education in a Suitcase, this received a positive response from participants. In this research project, it was recognized that there was "untapped potential" with regards to connecting this cryptocurrency project with broader philanthropic objectives.

Another use case in the education space is credential verification. Universities such as MIT in the US and McMaster University in Canada utilize Blockcerts, a digital credentialing system which can verify digital diplomas. Upon completion of a degree, students provide their blockchain address, which is then associated with the credential and stored immutably on the blockchain. This can save considerable time that would otherwise go to verifying and reprinting diplomas.

Supply Chain Tracking

Tracking goods as they move around the world is growing in complexity, and more people are demanding transparency to ensure that what they are

---

[85] SuperRare "Collect SuperRare Digital Artworks."
[86] Lentin et al., "From Smileys to Smileycoins."

purchasing has been ethically and sustainably sourced. Supply chain systems can integrate blockchain technology to provide visibility and transparency by providing a trusted and tamper-proof record for all parties. For example, the blockchain can be used to confirm that a fish that is being purchased at the supermarket can easily be traced back to its point of origin, ensuring that it has been sustainably sourced.[87] Existing infrastructure may take days to trace this information, but a blockchain system can provide this information in seconds.

Impact Collaboration

There is significant potential for blockchain technologies to align incentives with specific behaviours in more flexible ways. For example, platforms can fund activities, confirm activities have been carried out, and issue payments, all in an automated and decentralized way. For instance, cryptocurrency could be pledged for the fulfillment of a project, and upon confirmation the reward could then be released. An example of this is a platform like Impactio which provides a structured incentive system to connect funders, experts, and project leaders to collaborate to advance the UN's Sustainable Development Goals.[88] Projects can be submitted and subject matter experts are incentivized to provide feedback to improve. Any barriers to the deployment of a project are identified and incentives are distributed to resolve them. The entire process from proposal, review, and funding is automated, streamlined, and helps to surface projects that might not otherwise be considered as part of traditional grant review processes.

Looking Ahead and Staying up to Speed

Though the internet has been available to the world since the 1990s, new use cases continue to emerge as new technologies are developed, connected, and integrated. Similarly, uses for cryptocurrencies and blockchain

---

[87] IBM, "Sustainable Seafood Gets a Boost from IBM Blockchain Technology."

[88] Consensys, "Impactio: Blockchain Case Study for Philanthropy & Sustainability."

technology will continue to emerge for nonprofits as they continue to be actively developed and explored.

Many of the models described throughout this book have emerged in just the last few years. Organizations will need to continue adapting to new and emerging developments in the crypto space. In addition to examining and applying fundraising models, building organizational capacity and willingness to innovate, explore, and experiment will ensure that you are prepared to assess and adapt to any changes.

Ongoing professional development and education is important to stay informed and many resources can often be found via fundraising associations, conferences, and courses. However, if you find that there is a lack of offerings related to cryptocurrency, an email to your local association can help planning committees understand that there is demand for this information. Another organization that can help you stay ahead of the curve is NTEN, a community of nonprofit professionals dedicated to using technology to make the world a better place.[89]

Crypto Philanthropy

In late 2017, the Toronto crypto community raised over $200,000 in Ether donations for Covenant House through the Merry Merkle event during the December holiday season.[90, 91]

---

[89] NTEN, "NTEN."

[90] Powell, "Cryptogiving.ca 2019 Pre-Budget Submission."

[91] Bent, "MerryMerkle."

Get the Gift Checklist

- [ ] Evaluate your case for support and determine which type of crypto donor it might connect with
- [ ] Build a marketing plan that includes how you will promote your new program and how it will be integrated into the different parts of your fundraising program
- [ ] Develop a prospect research strategy using crypto-specific sources
- [ ] Create donor profiles for potential prospects
- [ ] Research crypto foundations with granting programs
- [ ] Develop a stewardship plan for crypto donors—it may differ from your current stewardship activities
- [ ] Launch your program as per your marketing plan
- [ ] Regularly evaluate the success of your program and adjust your strategies accordingly

CONCLUSION

> *"Dream big—you have nothing to lose, especially as cryptocurrency gains massive steam in the financial world."*
>
> - Henah Parikh, Development and Communications Manager at She's the First

There are natural curves to the adoption of all new technologies. In 1995, there were 16 million internet users. Today, there are over 4.1 billion.[92] While we may no longer think twice about sending an email to the other side of the world, this was not commonplace in the early 90s. The notion of a smartphone as we know it was introduced less than 15 years ago and in just that short period of time, our world has been transformed. As we write this, satellites are being launched into space to build a planetary network of broadband internet which will make connectivity even easier in remote areas.

As we look ahead to the future, just as the internet has allowed charities to transform the important work that is done around the world, cryptocurrencies will usher in another wave of growth, transformation, and innovation. What we are currently experiencing is the foundation of something much bigger, and the future will likely be one in which we use cryptocurrencies and the underlying technology without really even thinking about it, similar to how we use mobile devices and the internet today.

In the end, what is important to remember is that technology is "always an actor in, but not a driver of, social change."[93]

---

[92] ITU, "Measuring Digital Development."

[93] Coates, "What Futurists believe."

Social change starts with people, and nonprofits play a crucial role in building and shaping the world that we wish to live in. Cryptocurrencies and blockchains, like everything else that we use, are merely tools to achieve our goals. As the technology evolves and grows, so will the opportunities for your organization. Our hope is that this book has encouraged you to accept our invitation to create the future together.

Interviews with Early Crypto Philanthropy Adopters

Crypto Donors

Andrew

Andrew is a donor from Texas. He has been in crypto since 2010 and works in crypto mining and as an investor in both the crypto and traditional sectors.

What made you want to make a donation in Bitcoin? Who did you donate to?

I donated to BitGive and also to Binance Charity. For BitGive, they were one of the first charities that was trying to take advantage of the crypto space exclusively. I was excited to support a charity that exists, survives, and flourishes based on the crypto space and cryptocurrencies as donations. For Binance, there was a fundraiser that was run in SoHo during one of the Consensus conferences two years ago in New York. It was a large fundraising event that raised quite a bit for charitable programs in Africa.

What types of causes are you passionate about?

The overarching category is anything that has to do with freedom. Freedom of religion, freedom of speech, things of that nature.

Do you consider yourself a Libertarian? Bitcoin Maximalist? Decentralist?

It would be some portion of Bitcoin Maximalist, although not to the full extent. Definitely elements of that. It's possible that something supercedes or replaces Bitcoin. If it does a better job than what Bitcoin tries to do . . . but I just haven't seen that yet, and all current attempts haven't risen to that level, so from that standpoint, I have a large maximalist outlook on Bitcoin. But not 100% like some people, I look at everything. My political views are a mix of conservative and libertarian. Some issues are more libertarian, some more conservative. I couldn't really tell you the exact breakdown, but I would say it's primarily libertarian.

Do you donate to charities that don't have BTC donation programs?

Yes, and I would fall into the major donor category. I always think I could do more, but compared to the general population, I believe I give more than average. I'm drawn to these organizations by their causes and my belief systems. I want to give back from having done pretty well, and this is one of the ways to do that, through charitable donations. I don't like charities that immediately sell the crypto. If they're going to do that then I might as well donate fiat. It's possible that if there were a charity overseas, using traditional banking doesn't make sense, especially with smaller amounts. It's more effective to donate crypto.

Do you believe the crypto community is inherently philanthropic?

Yes—everybody I've met is philanthropic. There are some that are not, but I think at least up to this point, people have been more philanthropic.

Do you like to be publicly recognized for your gifts?

I prefer a more anonymous style of giving. I don't like the publicity portion of it—that's not why I do it. Sometimes I do let my name be known. We had a fundraiser for an old colleague who passed away and his family was raising funds to set up a memorial fund for one of his causes. To encourage others from our circles to donate, I was okay with my name being used then, for a very narrow and very specific reason. But for Binance Charity, I explicitly remained anonymous. For BitGive I asked to stay anonymous as well. For crypto donations, I do want to remain anonymous because I want to maintain a lower profile to not have my name pop up anywhere for security reasons.

What is one thing charities can do better to attract crypto donors?

I think that what would resonate are charities whose causes resonate with the current crowd of crypto people—which isn't everything. Going forward, as soon as charities see the latest successes in fundraising, they will adopt all of this—it's just a matter of time. Those charities whose missions and what they work on resonate with the current mindset, those can benefit if they plug into the space, because the people will be more willing to support because it lines up with their values and what they care about. More general donations will be tightly linked to mainstream adoption of crypto. I think it will happen outside of the US first. We see this in places where people are suffering from bad monetary policies, Argentina, Venezuela . . . and also for remittances. I want to see what Jack Dorsey is working on in Africa. Since he's very pro-Bitcoin, I wouldn't be surprised if we see a larger adoption there because of his effort. In other places where they have collapsing currency, there's a huge opportunity. Charities that work there and support those causes are at the forefront to benefit from it.

Do you think crypto will globalize the charity fundraising market?

Yes, definitely, for two particular reasons. First, for smaller amounts that are inconsequential on your taxes, people would donate because it's easier than through the banks. Secondly, we've had a few enormous catastrophes, like the tsunami, where the whole world comes together. For super catastrophic events, people would be willing to do crypto without much regard to what the taxable treatment is. Besides those two main points, it's difficult because of the recording and classifying for taxes. We need worldwide uniformity—we suffer from different jurisdictions.

Alejandro

Alejandro is a crypto donor from Greece. He works at a well-known cryptocurrency exchange and has been in crypto since 2013.

What made you want to donate with Bitcoin?

I was in Brazil at a conference when I met someone from BitGive [the first Bitcoin nonprofit]. They were helping people get the basic necessities in Venezuela. I have family there, so it was a cause I was very passionate about. I was thrilled to have made the donation. Then they wanted to publicly use my name and I said no—don't use my name.

Do you feel more connected to charities that accept crypto?

Absolutely! I grew up in Greece where they had issues with high inflation. We have to stock our refrigerator with food because at the end of the month your salary wasn't worth very much anymore, so you couldn't buy as much food. This type of inflation—price inflation—is a symptom of when too much money is printed. When the quantity of circulating currency increases—sometimes it shows in the prices of food and sometimes in the prices of real estate as we see in the US. The money printing right now is unprecedented. I believe that the monetary systems we have will be replaced. Will it be Bitcoin or something else? I don't know, but the way we store value will change.

Why is this new form of money so important?

Money is communication. Money is language. It's the first time we have this technology, but technology is neutral. I can use a knife to cut food or to hurt someone. It's not about the technology, it's the philosophy behind it. Bitcoin is a new form of doing things. It's scarce. It means I can't steal your money while you sleep.

Do you consider yourself a Libertarian?

I don't like labels, but if people want to consume something that's their own choice, but don't go drive and don't go near a school. I believe more in axioms, that a society needs underlying morals that we all agree to and those axioms are encoded in law. For example, I don't hurt other people - first, because it is immoral, and second because it is illegal, not the other way around. Libertarians try to create a utopia, but it's not always realistic.

What makes crypto donors unique?

It starts from the core philosophy. A lot of the people who are in crypto question the way we do things. They're always sensitive to how we can make money faster and safer. With Bitcoin, you know exactly where your money went and you can track it. You can't have multiple intermediaries as a part of the process. When you write a cheque to a charity, you have no idea. Crypto donors are more aware and more involved. They don't just donate to make themselves feel better, they want to be involved in the change.

Is the crypto community philanthropic?

Absolutely the crypto community is philanthropic. We haven't seen anything yet. It's only the beginning of how efficient the transfer of money can be. Today, if you want to donate to St. Jude Hospital in the US, but you live in Montenegro, you can't send a donation. It's not even very difficult, it's impossible. All charities should establish crypto donation programs to capture a global donation market. And they should get an expert to help them do it.

Michael Tozoni

Michael Tozoni was one of the founding members and Treasurer of Bitcoin100, a charitable fund that was created to encourage adoption among nonprofits. Michael managed the fund from 2011 to 2016 and helped to facilitate the donation of 681 BTC to 83 nonprofit organizations during that time.

How did you first get involved in cryptocurrency?

What got me interested was the idea of seasteading, the notion that rather than figuring out how to change government, we just set up these new ships that are like small city-states out in the water, and they can run their own governments or even have no government. And the idea at the time was, well, how do we handle the money problem? Because we can't really use gold.

All of these things are in the ocean, you can't really ship gold back and forth. So when you're ordering online, we need to use some sort of money. The problem is that if we use dollars or credit cards, we could be locked out. I was following the author of an online comic at the time and this guy just happens to mention Bitcoin and Twitter—this was in 2011—so I went to look into it and ended up spending the next two weeks reading all about it and realized that this would be perfect for seasteading, and it kind of dropped me down the rabbit hole.

I had also been involved with [the multiplayer, open-world video game] Second Life and had been playing around with digital currency since about 2003. Second Life had an in-game currency so that you could use it to hire people or sell your stuff. People would make furniture, apartments, clothing, even some software that could make doors open and elevators move around.

There was also gambling and a fledgling banking and stock market. However, the servers were in California and the government stepped in because of the gambling that was going on, so that was shut down. After the game banned all the casinos, which were some of the biggest businesses at the time, people were pulling their money out of the banks as well, and all the stock markets failed. So basically everybody who had invested was withdrawing everything and there was a massive economic crash. There was a run in the bank and some of them were accused of running Ponzi schemes because some of them were using fractional reserves.

When I found Bitcoin, it was a very simple thing to adopt, and I didn't have an issue with what's backing it because I know that value comes from just the value [of] people using it. And at the same time I realized that one of the benefits is that nobody can step in and say, "no you can't do that."

What was the intent behind Bitcoin100?

The general idea was that, at the time, Bitcoin was associated with drugs and hackers. And we wanted to give people something else that Bitcoin could be used for, and in this case, charity.

How was it received by the community when it was first launched?

Pretty good. We got a lot of people donating a lot of money pretty quickly. A lot of money at the time was $3,000.

Reflecting back on the experience, what were some of the highlights of the Bitcoin100?

The reason it was called Bitcoin100 was because if a charity was interested, we would help set up a way to accept Bitcoin and we would make a first donation of 100 bitcoin. Within maybe half a year, we had to change that to a thousand dollars because a hundred bitcoin was about $1,000 by then, but then it became considerably more. The reception was pretty good. Because Bitcoin grew in value, all the initial investments ended up being worth quite a bit.

In total, we gave to over 90 different charities. So effectively on the first maybe $3,000 [in] Bitcoin to the fund, we ended up giving up about a hundred thousand dollars' worth to all these charities.

Were there any surprises along the way?

At first, it was very hard to convince organizations to do it, and that's why we ended up with all these really random charities. Nobody really knew what Bitcoin was. But, the main reason was to promote Bitcoin and to help spread the idea of what it was. In the old days, it was found that the majority of Bitcoin was actually used to give to charities or people would just send tips to one another. And that was a majority of use of Bitcoin.

How did you maintain transparency?

We had a single Bitcoin address that all of our accounting was done with, so any money you deposited, you'd be able to see it there, any money sent out at the time on the blockchain and you could add memos to transactions. Every transaction that went out would actually detail where it was spent so anybody can always go through and verify that their money was being spent correctly.

Reflecting back on Bitcoin100, what do you think the impact has been on the crypto space?

We had an impact on changing the narrative of what Bitcoin is used for, because we were able to donate over a hundred thousand dollars to almost a hundred different charities. It gave Bitcoin legitimacy way back when Bitcoin had absolutely zero legitimacy of any kind, back when nobody took it seriously, except the very, very early adopters.

What advice would you give to fundraisers who are looking to raise money from the crypto community?

Be as trustworthy as you possibly can. One way they solved that problem with Bitcoin100, we had a completely public Bitcoin address.

So if you're a public charity why not make all your accounting—at least the Bitcoin side of it—completely public so that people don't have to trust you. They can just look at the accounting in a blockchain, because Bitcoin makes that super easy.

Jim Carter III

Jim Carter III is a technologist who helped numerous charities adopt Bitcoin donations and is the Founder of Cause Hack.

How did you get involved in cryptocurrency?

It was primarily out of interest from being a general technologist, always being open to upcoming trends and what could be immediately useful for a project. It would have been around late 2016 and I started getting curious about setting up my first Bitcoin wallet and a Coinbase account to do a couple of test transfers and really see it in practice.

At one point for my agency, I needed to pay developers in Bitcoin to simplify life. At that point, I started thinking about how it could actually be a utility for anything that I was involved with. I was working with a lot of companies that had Stripe accounts and Stripe was beta testing accepting cryptocurrency as a payment method. I experimented with this and I thought, hey, for some of the charities that I'm involved with, I'll reach out to them.

The case to be made was that there may be generous cryptocurrency holders who may want to give a donation in crypto, and in working with Pencils of Promise, a charity I was involved with, they trusted me to implement it. So I got it all working, gave it a test, and we just sat on it for a little bit. Then the Pineapple Fund came about, and that accelerated the entire plan. The way that I was able to facilitate everything with the Pineapple Fund was because of my previous work with Pencils of Promise, so I knew immediately what could be done and how quickly it could all take effect.

What inspired you to connect the dots between cryptocurrency and charities?

I saw the thread on Reddit about the Pineapple Fund after someone from Pencils of Promise told me about it, and I saw the opportunity to help my favorite charity with something that I was experimenting with, and had already set up, and that really sparked my interest.

And after setting it up for one organization, I just saw that there were a lot more nonprofits that could be helped. As someone who is in technology who likes to support nonprofits, it is abundantly clear to me that very few nonprofits were equipped to pursue this. I realized this was an opportunity to see if I could just help at a bigger level. And that's when I started to help other organizations who were getting funded by the Pineapple Fund.

I think it was about seven or eight nonprofits that needed my assistance and I was able to help charities receive 10% of the whole fund.

What advice would you give to charities who are considering adopting cryptocurrency?

It's clear to me that being prepared was half the battle. In T. Harv Eker's *Secrets of the Millionaire Mind*, one of the principles is that it's great to give, but you have to be willing to receive when someone gives to you. Being in a state of openness to get something of value is almost equally as valuable as putting it back out into the world, in a sense.

If I wasn't ready for something, a big piece of it was, well, what can I do to actually get myself ready? So we don't have to invest in everything that comes our way, but at least trying enough to know if it's for us, or if it's for us in our future, is a lot better than being unaware of what we don't know. I'm a much bigger fan of being very aware and knowing what you don't know.

How did your assisting with cryptocurrency impact your relationship with the organization?

I was already really close to Pencils of Promise before all this came around. Of the things that you can contribute—your time, talent or treasure—we didn't really have the treasure, and time was sparse, but I do have talent.

My wife and I set out a goal that we wanted to be able to build a school. And that was about a $50,000 investment. And, you know, we set out, and created a campaign fundraiser and we said, this could take us two years, five years, ten years, who knows, but we're going to have fun on the journey. It turned out well when I helped Pencils of Promise get the $1 million Bitcoin gift from Pine—of course, that was not my money, I was very aware of that—but I knew I was a big part of it.

And that reinforced that you don't have to give the treasure. You can also just give your talent. However, even though Pine provided the opportunity, I knew that that wasn't really my money. It was just me being part of the part of the fund. However, in a wonderful turn of events towards the end of the Pineapple Fund campaign, one of the last email conversations I had with Pine, I got an email with the subject line, "Thank you."

Pine took the time to say how much they appreciated the effort that I put in to helping them advance their campaign and realized that it would have been incredibly hard for them to do it without someone like me to help those that needed it the most. So because of that, Pine wanted to give a $250,000 dollar donation in my name to any charity of my choice.

That was a really wonderful moment, and I realized that was exactly the opportunity I was looking for to finally be able to contribute that treasure. And that was a big awakening moment for me. I love technology and I've put a lot of effort into my passion and my craft for many years. And even though I've built successful businesses and I've been part of really big campaigns, this was probably the first time where I absolutely saw that focusing on what you love to do, caring about the impact that you're making, focusing on that impact, not necessarily on the income, and just knowing that it will follow, is really something that is possible.

I was always really close to Pencils of Promise, but after that whole series of events I can't tell you how many doors it's opened for me, how many new connections it's unlocked in my life and the strongest relationship with the nonprofit that I could ever ask for.

What do you see in the future for cryptocurrency and what are the opportunities?

As someone who's been in tech for over two decades, there's one thing that has always reigned supreme, and that is: organizations that are willing to experiment and try, even if they don't realize it yet, have the opportunities. It's important for nonprofits to invest early in technology and their staff.

It's very clear to me when you look at the data and you see the yields, those that are willing to experiment and try new things will benefit—people are willing to pay for convenience.

So the more convenient that you can make it for a donor or for an ambassador to support you and, whether it's, "Hey, I have this idea, will you support me in trying it with you," and being open to accepting that even though it might be a little scary. It's not always common that we get these opportunities, but to be willing to say, "Look, we took a risk and that risk did pay off," I think that's where the magic is.

I'm not necessarily the crypto investor, but I'm more of a futurist who is thinking of ways that technology can be used for good and it makes me really happy to be part of that story.

FUNDRAISERS

Tony Stewart

Tony Stewart is the CEO and Co-Founder of Us4Warriors, a California-based organization to support veterans and their families.

Tell us about your organization

Us4Warriors is a rag-tag bunch of folks who decided to dedicate our off time to helping military and veterans and their families thrive. Help them get over difficult scenarios. We live in a very populated area, a very expensive area, and if you do the math there are 1.2 million who are here from military veterans and families here in San Diego County. We started looking and there are so many areas that we can help with. One was food. Food had become, overnight, our primary focus—it was something that everyone was having a difficult time keeping up with—the grocery bill. So we started Food4Warriors, then we started other things as the needs progressed. Work4Warriors does interviews and training trying to help people get jobs.

The bottom line is, we help them live for a stronger life. We help them prosper for a brighter future. We want to get everyone to a self-reliance stage where they can aspire to their dreams.

When somebody transitions out of service, they don't get to that self-reliance point where they can aspire for dreams. They're trying to aspire to survive to get to that next chapter. We want to make it so they can do more things—and we've done that.

Why did you decide to launch a crypto donation program?

There's a publication called *Nonprofit Tech for Good* and I frequent that to learn a little more about stuff that's trending. When I was looking through it I saw some interesting information about cryptocurrency. I knew nothing about cryptocurrency myself, but it just seemed like this was the new frontier. I said "Hey—let's do this."

How did you set up your program? Which currencies do you accept?

The Giving Block helped me out—they helped set it up and it was very easy, but at the same time it was litigious in a good way, because you want it to be sound. That really helped me, knowing that I had to go through some hurdles, a little bit more than a regular bank account. That reinforced the protective nature so I could talk with my board and convince the board to make the plunge as well. That's always the conversation—when it comes to nonprofits you have a board. You need to convince at least two thirds to move forward in a territory like this. There were a few folks who were a bit older sitting on the board and I had to convince a little bit. But some of the research that I did and the presentation that I gave to the board, everyone was reassured and all their questions were answered. Now everybody is loving it—it's a good thing!

Have you received any extraordinary gifts?

Recently, we got a couple thousand that just popped up out of nowhere. That's a big gift for us. Primarily, the gifts have been smaller and through campaigns like 'crypto for poker' or we did one that was a gaming contest and we got $1000 from that. More and more, we gain a lot of attention, where it has become somewhat of a stream to where every month we get something, and sometimes it outperforms other channels. During COVID-19, it's been really difficult. All of the fundraising events that we run normally that bring in five-digit figures, we haven't been able to do any of it. That was a tremendous loss. There was a point where the board was coming together wondering how we were going to make it through. We were going to have to shut things down. We were at the point where our Food4Warriors program was essential, but we couldn't get the money to pay for everything to help the thousands that we do, so it was challenging. We got some of those smaller amounts collectively from crypto and because of that, we were able to come back to the table and say, "we're going to come out of this." If it weren't for crypto . . . we're a small organization compared to many, and it was very challenging, but we're still here and we're thriving now.

What makes crypto donors differ from the typical people who give to your organization?

One thing I noticed about the crypto community is that there are a lot of outlaws in there. I mean that in a favourable way—everyone's a bit rogue. Some people will find out about the cause, and they're like, "We'll show up the rest of the world, and we'll give." There's a challenge to show the rest of the world that crypto is here to stay, it can make a difference, and that anyone can be a part of it. That's the thing about it that I see with the community. You may think they're the type of people who won't give anything—they're HODLING—and then all of a sudden, you get a tweet and someone drops some cash your way. Twitter is amazing—it's the call to action place for crypto. There's a lot of different social media we use, but when it comes to crypto, Twitter is the bugle horn.

Crypto Lingo

'HODL' ⟶ The origin of the term HODL comes from a forum post where a user made a typo when posting a rant about their strategy to buy and hold their bitcoin vs. trading it. HODL now represents that strategy, but has morphed to be an acronym for 'Hold On for Dear Life'—a joke around Bitcoin's price volatility.

What was the most challenging part of setting up a program?

The learning curve is really hard in the beginning. More of a learning curve for me, at my stage of life, than maybe someone a lot younger than me, where crypto is just part of their life. There are a lot of things in the beginning I had to figure out. No matter how many times someone tells you something, until you get your fingers in it, until you start seeing it, the repetition . . . you start adapting.

The accounting piece is sometimes a challenge. When it comes to taxes and accounting, and when it's anonymous, how do you deal with that? The anonymous gifts we've had have been low enough that it doesn't matter. Sometimes I want the whale,[94] but I'm also scared of the whale in case they make a huge gift and they say, "You can't tell anyone who I am." But now we have a policy. Those were the challenges I needed to learn.

Do you see crypto as a key element of your fundraising program?

Yeah, I would say almost two thirds of the fundraising comes from crypto. We're a small organization, but we're in five digit figures of crypto, so we feel pretty good. We keep working it, but it's generally small amounts on top of small amounts. We know that it's going to get better. After we get past all the COVID stuff, we have a podcast and we're going to be doing more educational stuff about crypto for military folks.

What advice would you give to other organizations thinking of starting their own programs?

Get some help from people that know... I may have waited longer in order to put it together myself. It might have taken a whole other year. The biggest thing I want to share is how excited we are about it. We want to turn Crypto4Warriors into much more than just a donation page. We want

[94] The term 'whale' refers to a person who holds a lot of cryptocurrency. Whales are some of the wealthiest people in the industry.

to have education for people as a part of our Prosper4Warriors. People don't get taught how to handle their money in general. There's no difference here. Especially for my area, for military and veterans, I think that I owe it to them to say, "Hey—here's this new frontier, you don't have to be left behind because you spent all this time at sea or deployed, and you didn't have the opportunity to learn because you were defending your country."

I want to be able to educate and help people—and help them prosper. Crypto is helping us do that.

Henah Parikh

Henah Parikh is the Development and Communications Manager at She's the First, an organization that teams up with local groups to make sure girls are educated, respected, and heard.

Why did you decide to launch a crypto donation program?

Originally, we hadn't considered a cryptocurrency donation program, but right after COVID-19 hit, individual donations plummeted. This was especially challenging because we are a grassroots organization so those one-time and monthly gifts from grassroots donors were vital. Once we learned more about the potential for cryptodonations around COVID relief, we knew it was a chance we could not pass up.

Which cryptocurrencies do you accept?

At this time, we accept a variety of tokens including Bitcoin, Ether, Zcash, and BAT.

Have you received any extraordinary gifts?

YES. Within eight weeks of getting us up for cryptocurrency donations, we received $42,000+ in gifts from event sponsorships and COVID relief initiatives. So far, these crypto donations are our second highest donor this year. That funding enabled us to release rapid funds to our global partners, which ensured mentors can reach 6,139 girls, delivered food, water, and menstrual kits to 1,439 girls and their families, and adapted education materials and methods reaching 6,810 girls.

What makes crypto donors different from the typical people who give to your organization?

To be honest, we actually don't know any contact information for most crypto gifts we've received, so they've been fully anonymous. This is somewhat challenging as it's harder to sustain that funding pipeline if we don't know who's given. Most generally, I've been surprised and touched by how generous crypto donors are with their gifts.

What was the most challenging part of setting up a program?

Crypto is still very . . . cryptic to folks. It took a steep learning curve for the team, our board, and our larger community to understand its potential and how cryptocurrency and crypto donations work.

Do you see crypto as a key element of your fundraising program?

Especially in a year when we've had to think creatively about new fundraising and income streams, absolutely. We're still learning and growing, but we do try to keep this cryptocurrency avenue in our mind when we think about fundraising strategies, social media, etc. For example, for Giving Tuesday this year, we've secured a match for donations which we'll extend to the crypto community as well.

What advice would you give to other organizations thinking of starting their own programs?

The first piece of advice is: don't discount the potential of crypto. Having a partner set us up with accepting cryptocurrency was 100% one of the best decisions we made; our annual investment in them has already paid for itself 10 times over, and it gave us a sense of peace and security to know this has all been vetted and done correctly by folks who know the crypto world inside and out.

The second piece of advice is that, as I mentioned, many donors will be anonymous, so being mindful that it may not be a sustainable source of revenue 100% of the time, but that many donors are extremely generous with their digital currency and so don't limit the possibilities of what can happen! Dream big—you have nothing to lose, especially as cryptocurrency gains massive steam in the financial world.

FUNDRAISING PLATFORMS

Connie Gallippi

Connie Gallippi is the Founder and Executive Director of BitGive, an innovative donation platform for nonprofits to provide transparency and accountability to donors by sharing financial information and direct project results in real-time.

You've been a true pioneer in crypto giving. Where did the idea for BitGive come about?

When I first learned about Bitcoin early on in 2011, it was really obscure. There was an event for the Bitcoin Foundation—it was the first event about Bitcoin. It was really quite a magical event because it brought everyone together to talk about Bitcoin. Being there, I really began to understand that this was going to be huge. I was inspired by what I thought was the future and I still believe is the future. There were engineers, investors, and some of the earliest startups in the space.

My role before BitGive was to help environmental nonprofits find funding. I was working as a consultant for creating state programs to support nonprofits. So I married these skills—my love of Bitcoin and my work with nonprofits. It was a pretty magical moment, looking back on it. I realized that if we could capture just a small fraction of the value that will be created by this industry to do good, it would have an incredible impact. The scale would be global—because Bitcoin is global. Imagine what we could do—we could actually move the needle, creating global empowerment using this technology.

I got excited and when I shared the idea to create a philanthropic platform for Bitcoin, others thought it was a good idea too. I ran with it, and now it's been seven years.

Tell me all about BitGive today and where you hope to take it.

Today we've come a long way—we celebrated seven years! We have GiveTrack, which is a platform we built, not just for donations, but to actually leverage the technology itself. There are a few solutions out there to just make Bitcoin donations. What we built is a whole platform on top of the Bitcoin blockchain and we're using a second layer solution called RSK, which is kind of like Ethereum, but built on the Bitcoin blockchain. The whole platform leverages the technology itself in the sense that when donations are made, if they're already in crypto, they stay in crypto, and if they're in fiat, we convert them into crypto. It's the opposite of what everyone else is doing, taking crypto and cashing it out immediately. We're using crypto and following it on the blockchain, to benefit from being able to transfer funds globally much cheaper, faster, and more transparently.

We've built a visualization for people to actually see their money going from wherever it comes from going into a charity's wallet. Knowing they actually received the money and then seeing what happens to it from there when they start to implement the projects donors gave towards.

It's very different because it's project-oriented. You can be transparent and say "this is what we're going to use the money for." Instead of it being a generic donation mechanism where you don't know where the money goes because it's been converted into fiat.

What were some of the challenges in getting your program set up?

In the earliest days, everything was a challenge. Bitcoin was so new, there was no path to follow, no model to look at, no regulatory guidance, there was nothing. Setting up a nonprofit and jumping through those hoops was new to me. We filed to get our tax exemption, which was an interesting request to the IRS to give a Bitcoin nonprofit a tax exemption. But we got it in 2014! And they hadn't even put out guidance at that point.

We had all those early challenges and when it came to building GiveTrack, we had a whole new set of challenges. How do you build a platform that does everything we want it to do? There are regulatory issues in terms of converting funds. Then you have to keep everything in crypto, there's volatility, and then track it on the blockchain and be able to visualize that and explain what it means. Anybody can look at a blockchain tracker, but they're not going to know what's happening. We were trying to really bring that forward in a way that's understandable to a mainstream donor and the public. All of those things have been challenging, but the biggest ones have been regulatory challenges. It's so hard to do what we want to do without jumping through all the hoops to get licenses, which costs millions of dollars. Why would a nonprofit spend millions of dollars to get licenced to be a money transmitter or money services business?

We'd love to be able to take credit cards and have mainstream people come and use the platform. But the conversion from a credit card to Bitcoin is not the easiest thing in the world. We have an amazing integration with Uphold. They enable us to accept 60 different crypto and fiat currencies, but there's a lot of friction because you have to sign up with Uphold first. For someone who wants to donate $20, they're not going to do that.

How are crypto donors different from regular donors?

Crypto people are a different breed in and of themselves. The crypto space tends to be people who are either very tech-leaning or very interested in decentralized systems, and systems that are outside of the government and traditional legacy institutions. Or they got involved in 2017 because they thought they could make a bunch of money. It's a unique set of people.

I think from a donor standpoint and what charities should be thinking is that it's a completely different demographic than what they would normally be appealing to. They need to appeal to tech-oriented people, younger people, males . . . that are typically not your normal donor.

Sometimes when the price spikes, if they're smart, and they have a lot of gains, they know they can offset it by donating, then you're going to be on their good side to help them out with that.

What do crypto donors look for in the charities they give to?

Some of the really obvious things are charities that appeal to the early core crowd. Things that are supporting people that have been wronged by their governments. Like Edward Snowden, or WikiLeaks. Government cut off donations to WikiLeaks because they were putting out information that the government didn't want out. So they started raising a lot of money in Bitcoin. The Electronic Frontier Foundation, the Internet Archive, organizations that help us establish an ecosystem outside of government.

When we started BitGive, we felt that Bitcoin was controversial enough, and we had enough of an uphill battle as it was. We wanted to stay outside of those controversial things. We've been doing things in public health, environment, and education, and they seem to be doing well. If we have tech-oriented things, they like those best because they are tech-leaning donors. It's across the board, but it does lean towards more of the government-related issues.

What are some of the projects you've been working with?

We have 24 different nonprofits we've worked with across 22 countries. One of the groups we've been working with is Code to Inspire. It's an amazing organization. Fereshteh Forough, the founder, is a refugee who started a school in Afghanistan for girls to teach them how to code. I love what they're doing. We raised funds for them to buy really high-performance computers so they can teach the girls graphic design.

We've done quite a few water projects in different countries in Africa including Kenya and most recently in Ethiopia, with the Canadian organization Run for Water. We helped them raise money for water in a town called Waraba where they piped fresh water into the community and into homes and schools and churches. Now the whole community has fresh spring water.

We worked with The Water Project—we have three different projects with them in Kenya. Building water wells, building rainwater capture basins, doing sanitation, and replacing latrines. We have three that just closed out their fundraising in Venezuela to support children and hospitals. They're dealing with a lot in Venezuela.

We launched our own COVID-19 relief fund benefitting three different organizations, one for direct relief for medical workers, one through GiveDirectly, which does cash transfers to vulnerable populations, and lastly with One Fair Wage, a US-focused organization for cash transfers to hourly workers. We also launched one with Save the Children México for food relief and hygiene packages for families in Mexico.

What advice can you give to fundraisers looking to raise money from the crypto community?

The thing we try to push our nonprofit partners on is that they have to reach out to donors, it's not just about putting up a program and hoping the donors will just donate to you. You have to put the effort in, just like traditional donors. Crypto donors also like to see that you're also using the tech, not just cashing out the tokens.

Alex Wilson

Alex Wilson is the CEO and Co-Founder of The Giving Block, a US-based crypto giving platform that helps charities fundraise within the crypto community.

Tell me about how you got involved in cryptocurrency.

I started when I was in a consulting job. When early 2017 came around, every Fortune 500 company wanted to do something with blockchain. I started developing blockchain education materials at my day job. On the weekends, I started investing in Bitcoin and trading crypto, and getting caught up in the hype. I've never turned back since then. In 2017, the bull market led Pat and I to start The Giving Block, seeing that real need for nonprofits to be able to accept crypto.

You work with a number of charitable organizations. What are some of the charities who have gotten on board with crypto?

We work with 50-60 organizations, with more coming on board every week. Some of the largest ones we work with include No Kid Hungry, Save the Children, and Pencils of Promise. We're working with all sizes of charities, but we're seeing the best ROI for nonprofits in the mid-to large-size organizations, typically over $1 million in annual revenue. Most of this comes back to a charity's online and social media presence. We're finding more alignment and better ROI with more established charities.

What are the characteristics of the charities you work with that make them particularly suited to having a crypto fundraising program?

A major one is just being flexible. Charities that are able to pivot quickly, work with their marketing teams to get messaging out, and actively engage with the crypto community will see a better ROI. For example, we didn't expect to run a COVID-19 campaign, but we quickly put together some partners and a marketing toolkit, and those that were able to pivot quickly and get that messaging out were the ones that did the best. Charities that are more passive, that accept crypto, but don't tell people about it, don't see as many donations.

What are some tips you can offer to charities to ensure their implementation is a success?

The main thing would be consistency. This is not a one-time announcement that you accept crypto and then you're done. You need to mix it into your regular messaging to donors to remind them that you are accepting crypto now. Remind them they can save money on their taxes in some countries by donating in crypto. Being consistent by messaging on a weekly or monthly basis makes a big difference.

What does The Giving Block do?

We try to make it as easy as possible for nonprofits to be able to accept crypto. On the back end for nonprofits, they get US Dollars in their account, so they don't have to worry about handling crypto or converting crypto, they don't even have to send tax receipts—it's all automated. All they have to do is transfer the money into their bank accounts. We handle the technical elements and marketing to drive traffic to the platform.

We're the only solution that's focused on nonprofits. There are other payment processors out there, but Giving Block is the only one that's built for nonprofits. We don't just provide the technical piece, but also the marketing to help charities drive donations.

What does the typical profile of a crypto donor look like?

The two main differences are, first, that they're much younger. A lot of the donors are Millennials or Gen Z, so in their twenties and thirties, which is almost the opposite of what a traditional donor looks like.

Secondly, they're very tech savvy. Part of that is because they're younger, but in general, most people using crypto right now, while it's not quite mainstream, are definitely on the tech-savvy side.

What advice can you give to fundraisers looking to raise money from the crypto community?

It's not as scary as you think. We get a lot of questions from board members or the executive team with common misconceptions around crypto. Questions like "isn't it just used for illegal activity?" The first thing is really doing some basic research and education on cryptocurrencies to debunk these misconceptions. Then people realize it's not as scary as it looks.

The market is bigger than a lot of fundraisers realize. We believe there are at least 70 million crypto users out there and the market cap for crypto is over $300 billion. They're often surprised to hear people have donated hundreds of millions of dollars in crypto. So it's not as new and scary as most people think and it's getting easier and easier to do.

What's the biggest crypto gift that you've seen on your platform?

The largest gifts have been six figures and our COVID-19 campaign raised over $1 million in aggregate, from a number of different donors.

BIBLIOGRAPHY

Banjo, Shelley, Kartikay Mehrotra, and William Turton. 2020. "TikTok's Huge Data Harvesting Prompts U.S. Security Concerns." *Bloomberg.* https://www.bloomberg.com/news/articles/2020-07-14/tiktok-s-massive-data-harvesting-prompts-u-s-security-concerns.

Bent, Rob. 2018. "MerryMerkle: How the Crypto Community Raised $200K for a Homeless Youth Shelter in 10 Days." *Medium.* https://medium.com/truebit/merrymerkle-how-the-crypto-community-raised-200k-for-a-homeless-youth-shelter-in-10-days-876477460f22.

Bitcoin. 2021. "Bitcoin Core integration/staging tree." GitHub. https://github.com/bitcoin/bitcoin.

Bitcoin Core. 2021. "Bitcoin Development." Bitcoin Core. https://bitcoin.org/en/development#code-review.

Bitcoin Pizza Index. 2021. "Bitcoin Pizza Index." Bitcoin Pizza Index. https://bitcoinpizzaindex.net/.

Bitcoin Wiki. 2021. "Satoshi (unit)." Bitcoin Wiki. https://en.bitcoin.it/wiki/Satoshi_(unit).

BitDegree. 2019. "Did You Know There are 861 Blockchains?" BitDegree. https://blog.bitdegree.org/did-you-know-there-are-861-blockchains-c60e1720fad5.

Blandin, Apolline, Gina Pieters, Yue Wu, Thomas Eisermann, Anton Dek, Sean Taylor, and Damaris Njoki. 2020. *3rd Global Cryptoasset Benchmarking Study.* Cambridge Centre for Alternative Finance. https://www.jbs.cam.ac.uk/wp-content/uploads/2020/09/2020-ccaf-3rd-global-cryptoasset-benchmarking-study.pdf.

Blockchain.com. 2021. "Bitcoin Explorer." Blockchain.com. www.Blockchain.com/explorer.

Blockchain.com. 2021. "Transaction Summary." Blockchain.com. https://www.blockchain.com/btc/tx/f6ec92785aac2bace9156d786a625666c3e11 3a50ccf4bdb535d175219a5f486.

Blumberg, Mark. 2020. "CRA asking about cryptocurrencies on charity audits." Canadian Charity Law. https://www.canadiancharitylaw.ca/blog/cra-asking-about-cryptocurrencies-on-charity-audits/.

Browne, Ryan. 2017. "Cryptocurrency market now worth $500 billion, more than Warren Buffett's Berkshire Hathaway." *CNBC.* https://www.cnbc.com/2017/12/13/cryptocurrency-market-now-worth-half-a-trillion-dollars.html.

Buterin, Vitalik, E. Glen Weyl, and Zoe Hitzig. 2018. "Liberal Radicalism: A Flexible Design For Philanthropic Matching Funds." *SSRN* 1, no. 1 (December): 37. https://papers.ssrn.com/sol3/papers.cfm?abstract_id=3243656.

CAGP. 2021. *Planned Giving for Canadians* (eBook). The Canadian Association of Gift Planners (CAGP). https://www.cagp-acpdp.org/en/civicrm/contribute/transact?reset=1&id=42.

Canadian Crypto. 2021. "Free Google Sheets Cryptocurrency Portfolio Tracker." CanadianCrypto.io. https://canadiancrypto.io/free-google-sheets-cryptocurrency-portfolio-tracker/.

Carpenter, Mark. 2020. "Salvation Army Hawaii lands generous 'crypto kettle' donation." *Hawaii News Now.* https://www.hawaiinewsnow.com/2020/12/23/salvation-army-lands-generous-crypto-kettle-donation/.

Cedrom. 2019. "BCV admite hiperinflación de 53.798.500% desde 2016." *Venezuela al Dia.* https://venezuelaaldia.com/2019/05/28/banco-central-venezuela-hiperinflacion-2016/.

Coates, Joseph, and Jennifer Jarratt. 1989. *What Futurists Believe.* Bethesda, MD: Lomond Publications Inc.

CoinMarketCap. 2020. "Total Market Capitalization." CoinMarketCap. coinmarketcap.com.

CoinTraffic. 2020. "Crypto Audience Revealed: Who Is Your Target User?" CBlog. https://cointraffic.io/blog/crypto-audience-revealed-who-is-your-target-user/.

Comben, Christina. 2019. "Google Analytics Reveal Surprising Bitcoin Demographics." *Bitcoinist.* https://bitcoinist.com/google-analytics-bitcoin-demographics/.

Connelly, Anne. 2019. "The Landscape of Cryptocurrency Donation Programs." Anne Connelly. https://www.anneconnelly.ca/s/The-Landscape-of-Cryptocurrency-Donation-Programs.pdf.

ConsenSys. 2021. "Impactio: Blockchain Case Study for Philanthropy & Sustainability." Blockchain for Social Impact. https://consensys.net/blockchain-use-cases/social-impact/impactio-case-study/.

ConsenSys. 2021. "Project Unblocked Cash: Blockchain Case Study for NGOs." ConsenSys. https://consensys.net/blockchain-use-cases/social-impact/project-unblocked-cash-case-study/.

Copeland, Tim. 2019. "The complete story of the QuadrigaCX $190 million scandal." *Decrypt.* https://decrypt.co/5853/complete-story-quadrigacx-190-million.

Cudo Donate. 2021. "Donate your idle computer time to Charity." Cudo Donate. https://www.cudodonate.com/.

De, Nikhilesh. 2019. "$66 Million Building to Be Tokenized on Ethereum Blockchain in Record Deal." *CoinDesk.* https://www.coindesk.com/66-million-building-to-be-tokenized-on-ethereum-blockchain-in-record-deal.

Doucette, Keith. 2019. "Tales from the crypto: Clients want to see human remains of QuadrigaCX founder." *Investment Executive.* https://www.investmentexecutive.com/news/industry-news/tales-from-the-crypto-clients-want-to-see-human-remains-of-quadrigacx-founder/.

Elliot, Francis, and Gary Duncan. 2009, January 3. "Chancellor Alistair Darling on brink of second bailout for banks." *The Times.*

https://www.thetimes.co.uk/article/chancellor-alistair-darling-on-brink-of-second-bailout-for-banks-n9l382mn62h.

Ethereum. 2021. "A digital future on a global scale." Ethereum. https://ethereum.org/en/eth2/vision/.

Fairley, Peter. 2019. "Ethereum Plans to Cut Its Absurd Energy Consumption by 99 Percent." *IEEE Spectrum.* https://spectrum.ieee.org/computing/networks/ethereum-plans-to-cut-its-absurd-energy-consumption-by-99-percent.

Gage, Phinneas. 2016. "Re: Bitcoin 100 has run its course. This is the rebate thread." BitcoinTalk.org. https://bitcointalk.org/index.php?topic=1659475.msg16668096#msg16668096.

Gitcoin. 2021. "$10,231,373 of Funding for Open Source Software." Gitcoin. https://gitcoin.co/results.

Gitcoin. 2021. "Gitcoin Grants." Gitcoin. https://gitcoin.co/grants/.

The Giving Block. 2021. "What is #BagSeason?" Bitcoin Tuesday. https://bitcointuesday.org/Top-10-Cryptocurrency-Donations-Bitcoin-And-Beyond.

Google. 2021. "Google Ad Grants." Google. https://www.google.com/grants/.

Gould, Jonathan. 2021. "OCC Chief Counsel's Interpretation on National Bank and Federal Savings Association Authority to Use Independent Node Verification Networks and Stablecoins for Payment Activities." Office of the Comptroller of the Currency. https://www.occ.gov/news-issuances/news-releases/2021/nr-occ-2021-2a.pdf.

Government of Canada. 2018. "Determining fair market value of non-cash gifts." Government of Canada. https://www.canada.ca/en/revenue-agency/services/charities-giving/charities/operating-a-registered-charity/issuing-receipts/determining-fair-market-value-gifts-kind-non-cash-gifts.html.

Hankin, Aaron. 2019. "Bitcoin Pizza Day: Celebrating the $80 Million Pizza Order." *Investopedia.* https://www.investopedia.com/news/bitcoin-pizza-day-celebrating-20-million-pizza-order/.

Harper, Colin. 2020. "Gemini Donates $50K to HRF to Help Fund Another Round of Bitcoin Developers in 2021." *CoinDesk*. https://www.coindesk.com/gemini-donates-50k-hrf-fund-bitcoin-developer-2021.

Helms, Kevin. 2020. "9 Countries Show Huge Growth in Cryptocurrency Interest: Coinmarketcap." Bitcoin.com. https://news.bitcoin.com/countries-growth-cryptocurrency-coinmarketcap/.

Huynh, Kim, Christopher Henry, Gradon Nicholls, and Mitchell Nicholson. 2020. "Benchmarking Bitcoin Adoption in Canada: Awareness, Ownership and Usage in 2018." *Ledger* 5, no. 1 (January): 1. https://doi.org/10.5195/ledger.2020.206.

IBM. 2020. "Sustainable Seafood Gets a Boost from IBM Blockchain Technology for Insight into the Journey from Sea to Table." IBM Newsroom. https://newsroom.ibm.com/2020-06-25-Sustainable-Seafood-Gets-a-Boost-from-IBM-Blockchain-Technology-for-Insight-into-the-Journey-from-Sea-to-Table.

IFAD. 2017. "Sending Money Home." The International Fund for Agricultural Development (IFAD). https://www.ifad.org/documents/38714170/39135645/Sending+Money+Home+-+Contributing+to+the+SDGs%2C+one+family+at+a+time.pdf/c207b5f1-9fef-4877-9315-75463fccfaa7.

ITU. 2019. "Measuring Digital Development." *ITU Publications*. https://www.itu.int/en/ITU-D/Statistics/Documents/facts/FactsFigures2019.pdf.

Kalra, Jaspreet. 2020. "Children's Heart Charity Receives $48K in Crypto Donations." *CoinDesk*. https://www.coindesk.com/childrens-heart-charity-receives-48k-in-crypto-donations.

Kelly, Jemima. 2018. "Anonymous bitcoin philanthropist donates $5 million to medicine foundation." *Reuters*. https://fr.reuters.com/article/uk-bitcoin-philanthropy/anonymous-bitcoin-philanthropist-donates-5-million-to-medicine-foundation-idUSKBN1FM2G4.

Khatri, Yogita. 2020. "BitMEX operator is donating $2.5M to coronavirus relief efforts." *Yahoo! Finance.* https://ca.finance.yahoo.com/news/bitmex-operator-donating-2-5m-111509619.html.

King, Alex. 2020. "Frozen Paypal account a nightmare for unemployed man; company now helping." *WTVQ.* https://www.wtvq.com/2020/05/27/paypal-working-help-customers-frozen-accounts/.

Local Bitcoins. 2021. "Local Bitcoins." Local Bitcoins. www.Localbitcoins.com.

Mann, Sonya. 2019. "Zcash Foundation Donation to Open Privacy." The Zcash Foundation. https://www.zfnd.org/blog/open-privacy-donation/.

Martin, Chris. 2020, Sept. 1. "'Getting paid to produce Bitcoins': Crypto miner is scoring 700% profits selling electricity to the grid." *Financial Post.* https://financialpost.com/technology/bitcoin-miner-is-scoring-700-profits-selling-energy-to-grid.

Meldrum, Andrew. 2006, Aug. 17. "Where a basketful of groceries costs a bucketful of cash." *The Guardian.* www.theguardian.com/business/2006/aug/17/Zimbabwenews.internationalnews.

Mizrahi, Avi. 2020. "Binance Donates $1 Million in Crypto for Australian Bushfire Relief." Bitcoin.com. https://news.bitcoin.com/binance-donates-1-million-in-crypto-for-australian-bushfire-relief/.

Monero. 2021. "Monero: A Private Digital Currency." Monero. https://www.getmonero.org/.

Morgan, Pamela. 2018. *Cryptoasset Inheritance Planning: A Simple Guide for Owners.* Merkle Bloom LLC. https://www.amazon.ca/Cryptoasset-Inheritance-Planning-Simple-Owners-ebook/dp/B07BRQ864J.

MtGox Team. 2014. "Mt Gox Announcement of February 17th, 2014." MtGox Team. https://web.archive.org/web/20140217113525/https://www.mtgox.com/img/pdf/20140217-Announcement.pdf.

Mushakavanhu, Tinashe. 2015. "I was a quadrillionaire in Zimbabwe, but could barely afford to buy bread." *Quartz.* https://qz.com/africa/426925/i-was-a-quadrillionaire-in-zimbabwe-but-could-barely-afford-to-buy-bread/.

Nonprofit Tech for Good. 2019. "Global NGO Technology Report 2019." Funraise. https://funraise.org/techreport.

NTEN. 2021. "NTEN." NTEN. https://www.nten.org.

Ogwu, Emmanuel. 2019. "Tether donates $1 million to help victims in hurricane Dorian-ravaged Bahamas." *Micky.* https://micky.com.au/tether-donates-1-million-to-help-victims-in-hurricane-dorian-ravaged-bahamas/.

Partz, Helen. 2019. "Pineapple Fund Writes Farewell Post, Reports That All Funds Have Been Donated." *Cointelegraph.* https://cointelegraph.com/news/pineapple-fund-writes-farewell-post-reports-that-all-funds-have-been-donated.

PayPal. 2020. "PayPal Launches New Service Enabling Users to Buy, Hold and Sell Cryptocurrency." PayPal Newsroom. https://newsroom.paypal-corp.com/2020-10-21-PayPal-Launches-New-Service-Enabling-Users-to-Buy-Hold-and-Sell-Cryptocurrency.

PND. 2018. "Silicon Valley Community Foundation Held Billions in Digital Assets." *Philanthropy News Digest (PND).* https://philanthropynewsdigest.org/news/silicon-valley-community-foundation-held-billions-in-digital-assets".

Post, Kollen. 2020. "Carnegie Mellon University Sees $4M Pledge to Develop DeFi Research Program." *Cointelegraph.* https://cointelegraph.com/news/carnegie-mellon-university-sees-4m-pledge-to-develop-defi-research-program.

Powell, Michael. 2019. "Cryptogiving.ca 2019 Pre-Budget Submission." *Cryptogiving.ca.* https://sencanada.ca/content/sen/committee/421/CSSB/Briefs/CSSB_ImpactCanada_e.pdf.

Power Ledger. 2021. "Energy Reimagined." Power Ledger. https://www.powerledger.io/.

Reitman, Rainey. 2011. "Bitcoin - a Step Toward Censorship-Resistant Digital Currency." The Electronic Frontier Foundation. https://www.eff.org/deeplinks/2011/01/bitcoin-step-toward-censorship-resistant.

@RhythmTrader. 2019. Twitter. https://twitter.com/Rhythmtrader/status/1168129091960221696.

Rizzo, Pete. 2014. "Mt. Gox Allegedly Loses $350 Million in Bitcoin (744,400 BTC), Rumoured to be Insolvent." *CoinDesk.* https://www.coindesk.com/mt-gox-loses-340-million-bitcoin-rumoured-insolvent.

Robitzski, Rob. 2018. "Charity Lets You Mine Monero to Post Bail." *IEEE Spectrum.* https://spectrum.ieee.org/tech-talk/computing/networks/cryptocurrency-charities-are-paying-off-disadvantaged-new-yorkers-bail.

Rooney, Kate. 2018. "Ripple gives away $29 million of its cryptocurrency to public schools." *CNBC.* https://www.cnbc.com/2018/03/28/ripple-gives-away-29-million-of-its-cryptocurrency-to-public-schools.html.

Shaw, Hollie. 2018. "No joke: KFC Canada starts accepting Bitcoin for a bucket of chicken, immediately sells out." *Financial Post.* https://financialpost.com/news/retail-marketing/no-joke-kfc-canada-starts-accepting-bitcoin-for-a-bucket-of-chicken-immediately-sells-out.

Sinclair, Sebastian. 2020. "Cryptocurrency CEO Donated Second-Largest Amount to Joe Biden's Campaign." *CoinDesk.* https://www.coindesk.com/cryptocurrency-ceo-donated-second-largest-amount-to-joe-bidens-campaign.

Smith, Ryan. 2021. "Good Samaritan Donates $280,000 in Bitcoin to WikiLeaks Defence Fund." *BeInCrypto.* https://beincrypto.com/good-samaritan-donates-280000-in-bitcoin-to-wikileaks-defence-fund/.

Stefansson, Gunnar, and Jamie Lentin. 2017. "From Smileys to Smileycoins: Using a Cryptocurrency in Education." *Ledger* 2, no. 1 (December): 1. https://doi.org/10.5195/ledger.2017.103.

Stoner, Joshua. 2020. "Polymath Launches 'Token Studio 2.0' on 'Polymesh' Digital Securities Blockchain." *Securities.io*. https://www.securities.io/polymath-launches-token-studio-on-polymesh/.

SuperRare. 2021. "SuperRare." SuperRare. https://superrare.co.

Tidy, Joe. 2020. "Mysterious 'Robin Hood' hackers donating stolen money." *BBC News*. https://www.bbc.com/news/technology-54591761.

u/pineapplefund. 2017. "I'm donating 5057 BTC to charitable causes! Introducing The Pineapple Fund." *Reddit*. https://www.reddit.com/r/Bitcoin/comments/7jj0oa/im_donating_5057_btc_to_charitable_causes/.

Vanek Smith, Stacey. 2018, June 19. "< The Measure Of A Tragedy." The Indicator from Planet Money. *NPR*. https://www.npr.org/transcripts/621563128.

Vulliamy, Ed. 2011, Apr. 3. "How a big US bank laundered billions from Mexico's murderous drug gangs." *The Guardian*. https://www.theguardian.com/world/2011/apr/03/us-bank-mexico-drug-gangs.

Wikimedia. 2012. "Diffusion of Ideas." Wikimedia. https://commons.wikimedia.org/wiki/File:Diffusion_of_ideas.svg.

Wikipedia. 2021. "Hyperinflation in Zimbabwe." *Wikipedia*. https://en.wikipedia.org/wiki/Hyperinflation_in_Zimbabwe#:~:text=In%20June%202008%20the%20annual,estimated%20at%2079%2C600%2C000%2C000%25%20per%20month.

Wikipedia. 2021. "Initial Coin Offering." *Wikipedia*. https://en.wikipedia.org/wiki/Initial_coin_offering#:~:text=The%20first%20token%20sale%20(also,%242.3%20million%20at%20the%20time.

Wikipedia. 2021. "Mt. Gox." *Wikipedia*. https://en.wikipedia.org/wiki/Mt._Gox.

Wikipedia. 2021. "Vitalik Buterin." *Wikipedia*. https://en.wikipedia.org/wiki/Vitalik_Buterin.

The World Bank. 2017. "The Unbanked." *Global Findex.* https://globalfindex.worldbank.org/sites/globalfindex/files/chapters/2017%20Findex%20full%20report_chapter2.pdf.

The World Bank. 2020. "Remittance Prices Worldwide." The World Bank. https://remittanceprices.worldbank.org/sites/default/files/rpw_report_september_2020.pdf.

The World Bank. 2021. "Personal remittances, received (current US$)." The World Bank. https://data.worldbank.org/indicator/BX.TRF.PWKR.CD.DT.

Wright, Turner. 2020. "Ethereum Foundation announces $3.8M in new grants." *Cointelegraph.* https://cointelegraph.com/news/ethereum-foundation-announces-38m-in-new-grants.

Young, Martin. 2020. "75 crypto exchanges have closed down so far in 2020." *Cointelegraph.* https://cointelegraph.com/news/75-crypto-exchanges-have-closed-down-so-far-in-2020.

Made in the USA
Columbia, SC
29 October 2021

48078533R00098